D1271243

The Dark Interval

TRANSLATED AND EDITED BY ULRICH BAER

Letters on Life: New Prose Translations

The Dark Interval

Letters for the Grieving Heart

Rainer Maria Rilke

BLOOMSBURY PUBLISHING
LONDON · OXFORD · NEW YORK · NEW DELHI · SYDNEY

BLOOMSBURY PUBLISHING
Bloomsbury Publishing Plc
50 Bedford Square, London, WC1B 3DP, UK

BLOOMSBURY, BLOOMSBURY PUBLISHING and the
Diana logo are trademarks of Bloomsbury Publishing Plc

First published in 2018 in the United States by Modern Library,
an imprint of Random House, a division of
Penguin Random House LLC, New York
First published in Great Britain 2018

A catalogue record for this book is available from the
British Library

ISBN: HB: 978-1-5266-0298-5; eBook: 978-1-5266-0296-1

2 4 6 8 10 9 7 5 3 1

Printed and bound in Great Britain by CPI Group (UK) Ltd,
Croydon CR0 4YY

To find out more about our authors and books visit www.
bloomsbury.com and sign up for our newsletters

My life is not this steeply sloping hour
Through which you see me hasten on.
I am a tree standing before my background
I am but one of many of my mouths
The one that closes before all of them.

I am the rest between two notes
That harmonize only reluctantly:
For death wants to become the loudest tone—

But in the dark interval they reconcile
Tremblingly, and get along.
    And the beauty of the song goes on.

RILKE, The Book of Hours (1905)

PREFACE

Throughout his life, the poet Rainer Maria Rilke addressed in direct and personal letters individuals who were close to him, who had contacted him after reading his works, or whom he had met briefly—anyone with whom he felt a kind of inner connection. At the time of his death in 1926 at the age of fifty-one, Rilke had written more than fourteen thousand letters, which the poet considered to be as significant as his poetry and prose. Especially for readers less familiar or comfortable with poetry, Rilke's letters offer original yet accessible thoughts on the role of love, death, and art in our lives.

Within this vast correspondence, there are about two dozen letters of condolence. In them, Rilke writes about loss and mortality, assuming the role of a sensitive and serious, yet ultimately uplifting guide through the unavoidably painful dimensions of life. These letters, gathered here into one volume for the first time, together tell a story leading from an unflinching acknowledgment of death to profound personal transformation. When read on their own, each of the letters may offer solace for anyone dealing with loss. They may likewise provide a blueprint for finding the right words to convey sympathy and compassion to those in mourning. What can you say in the face of loss, when words seem too frail and ordinary to communicate our grief and soothe the pain? These letters offer guidance in our effort to provide solace for the bereaved, and to not let loss and grief overwhelm, numb, and silence us.

Rilke believed that it was our responsibility to try to make sense of our condition and circumstances here on earth, rather than devote ourselves to imagining a realm of greater meaning where suffering may cease. He also distrusted the major political ideologies of the modern age, which provided comfort via collective identities, overarching causes, or abstract ideals. He thought the best we can do is to live fully, by which he meant being receptive to the richness of life, not only in easy times but also during "the dark interval," as a poem in *The Book of Hours* (1905) puts it, when life brings hardship and loss. It is possible to avoid a true awareness of the fact that life entails loss, that between the two notes of birth and death we pass through "the dark interval," which includes parting but ultimately contributes to life as a beautiful song. We can distract ourselves, cling to the words and teachings of others that gloss over our pain, or assume preformed identities via religion or ideology that spare us from the difficult and hard work of acknowledging and enduring suffering. But the price for such refusal, Rilke feared, was a less aware, less intensely lived life, or a life lived on someone else's terms. Not really confronting the presence of death would perhaps let us live a happy and stable life, in a conventional sense. But it would be a life that is less deep and—during the dark moments when we experience a loss or, if we ourselves are spared major afflictions, help others in mourning—ultimately less strong, or even feel less real.

The letters collected in this book are prompted in most cases by the death of a recipient's loved one. Rilke wrote most of them almost instantaneously after receiving the terrible news of someone's death, and in several of the letters you can feel this urgency from the very first line— Rilke all but skips a proper address and its formalities to leap right into the most difficult matter, which is the death mourned by the letter's recipient. At other times he takes a few sentences to make himself fully present to the other person so that he can be *with* them, through his language, when they are all alone. Time is critical when someone has lost a beloved person, and Rilke knew that an immediate response could lessen the terrible, gaping solitude that had opened up in someone's life. A condolence letter would not fill this loss. But if Rilke responded right away, the fact that he had thrown himself into confronting the death of

the beloved person head-on in his letter, rather than rely-
ing on conventional formulas of sympathy, meant a great
deal to those to whom he wrote. We know this because
these men and women cherished Rilke's letters like talis-
mans, the way one may keep love letters for a lifetime. Indeed, some of the letters sound so intimate and are so
strongly felt that they read like love letters, since Rilke
aims straight at the heart of his recipients with his unspar-
ing yet deeply empathetic exhortations to confront, acknowledge, and grow through grief. A few of the recipients
had been Rilke's lovers at earlier moments in his life. But
the intensity of love, or an intimacy shared by genuine
concern for the other's experience, is tangible in each letter. With these letters, Rilke presented the gift of enduring
language to people who had suffered and often been all but
reduced to silence by profound loss. His language lasted, in
the hands and memories of his recipients, and has now
been passed down to us, even after all of them have died
themselves.

For today's readers, these letters serve as models of how
to address a grieving person right away, without searching
long, often for too long, for the right words and appropriate
phrasing. There is something almost seductive about Rilke's letters. This impression is not due to lingering romantic feelings, but because Rilke aimed to bring the bereaved
back into communication, and coax them back into the

conversation that we call life, right at the moment when they felt most cut off from the world. He gave them words when those were lacking, and told them there is a way to articulate their pain even if that pain constricts their hearts and throats. These letters are gifts of language. But they are also more than that.

Rilke beseeches the addressee (and thus also us, since Rilke wrote his letters in the awareness and with the expectation that they were likely to be published later) not to evade the pain that life brings us. "Death does not *exceed* our strength," Rilke writes in one of these letters. He implores the recipient, who has just lost someone dear to her, not to withdraw from life out of fear of the nearly unbearable pain. Remain *in* life, Rilke exhorts her, continue to work on the many things the deceased person could not complete, touch the unspeakably mute and lifeless clothes and things, now heavy with grief, which the beloved person had so recently imbued with life. This is Rilke's unceasing counsel for those who have lost someone they love. Stay with your pain, and instead of shrinking away from it, use it to forge another path back into life.

Rilke's letters of condolence are both subtle and stern, and he remained skeptical about easy consolation. "Woe to those who have been consoled," Rilke quotes the early-twentieth-century and now all but forgotten French playwright Marie Lenéru in one of his letters. He cautions against consolation since it can be a diversion instead of healing, and because consolation can become a superficial and almost heartless admonition to get over the loss, to move on, and ultimately to forget. Time, writes Rilke, does not "console, as people say superficially, at best it assigns things to their proper place and creates an order." After the great stillness of loss, gradually life begins to become normal again. The hours and days swing back into their habitual rhythms, which were so violently disrupted by death. The grieving person has to eat, breathe, regain less fitful sleep, and the world and its people, which had been circling around the great stillness at an awkward distance, start to encroach again. But that is not consolation. The wound heals but it does not disappear. A stillness and an absence remain, which sometimes hurts unexpectedly.

A few of the letters were written after longer periods of thought. They tap into Rilke's lifelong reflection on what ways life is interlaced with loss, and how we can find meaning in life without simply assuming that death is its stark opposite. A greater meaning, encompassing both life and death alike, is usually found in realms available only through faith. But just as life is continually transformed through the rhythms of creation and loss, Rilke insisted that we are capable of transforming our experiences on earth into something new and inherently meaningful without recourse to faith. As a poet, Rilke used words like very few other writers not only to express experiences but to create distinct experiences for us. But all of us, and not only poets, have the capacity to transform our experiences of loss into a renewed awareness of life. How does Rilke know this? Because we have the capacity to love, where through the encounter with another person our life is transformed. Through love and through death, our innate ability to transform the loss of control is activated to bring forth a deeper awareness of life. Or, differently put, through love and death we learn that life entails the loss of self-control and the loss of others, and that a true awareness of this fact presses us more deeply into life.

This is why Rilke does not sugarcoat the necessary confrontation with pain in these letters but admonishes the recipients to use pain to reconnect with life. He wants the individuals to whom he speaks not to retreat into bitter loneliness but to recognize that life is also, and perhaps above all in the moments of intense pleasure and pain wrought on us by love and death, transformation. We should explore, as painful as it may be, in what specific ways a particular loss impacts our life. This will allow us to use our pain to transform our life actively, instead of being hopelessly subjected to inevitable suffering. Instead of denying death and loss, we ought to explore more deeply what life has to offer in *all* of its dimensions. We should gingerly explore where the borders between mental and bodily pain begin to blur, and become aware while suffering a loss—this is critical for Rilke—that the beloved person now lives on in our memories and daily conduct.

When my father died a painful death after a difficult and humiliating illness, I was at a loss for words. It was only a few weeks after the attacks of September 11, 2001, which I had experienced in downtown New York. Occasionally when I inhaled, now separated forever from my father who had lived and died at a considerable distance, in Germany, the air I drew into my lungs seemed still to reverberate with the tremors of the attacks. Weeks and months passed. But instead of allowing life to gradually run its normal course again, with the confidence that each new day would present me with many things—good and bad, but nothing that would overwhelm me—I had to make great efforts to have even one normal hour. Each morning after waking up, I was jolted back into the awareness and pain of my loss, as if finding myself back in a prison of pain from which sleep had allowed me to escape for a spell. For the rest of the time, during the days when the unusually beautiful fall weather in New York turned to a mild winter and then spring, I was on guard, ready to retreat at any moment from anything that would make me feel even a bit out of the ordinary, lest it would trigger another loss of control. There were very few moments during those numb days when I was not taut with apprehension of any intense emotion, and there were few moments—I realize only in retrospect—when I felt relaxed enough simply to be.

I looked for counsel, guidance, and consolation, but could not find much. Only in Rilke's letters did I discover the empathic attention that I needed. During this long period of disequilibrium, when I feared that consciously lived life was going to slip forever out of reach—a life of choices made deliberately yet boldly, and in keeping with my true self—I grasped at these letters for support. It says perhaps something about me that I could connect with a writer very far away when I couldn't connect easily to the people nearby or to the professionals devoted to helping me to come to terms with my loss. But I tend to think that Rilke's letters said something absolutely unique that nobody else had the courage or wisdom to share.

I did not understand very much of what the poet had written to long-forgotten people nearly a hundred years earlier. How was pain going to lead me more deeply *into* life, when my fear of new upheaval kept me from being open to any experience—including positive ones—since I could not hope to control them? I read and reread Rilke's letters. I felt less alone, and the letters slowly led me to think that my pain was maybe not something to be overcome but rather a way forward into life. Over a period of many months, they guided me in the direction of actual life, that daily life of surprises and the unknown from which I had withdrawn out of fear. I had been on my way to shutting myself off from experiencing anything, lest it overwhelm me. Rilke's words became companions and signals directing me back into life.

In particular, there was a passage from one of Rilke's letters from the year 1908 that I had stumbled upon, quite by accident, in an old book shortly after my father's death. I read these words out loud, in a dazed state and through tears, at my father's funeral. Then I started repeating them over and over like a mantra:

> But as to the influence of the death of someone near on those he leaves behind, it has long seemed to me that this ought to be no other than a higher responsibility. Does the person who passes away not leave all the things he had begun in hundreds of ways to be continued by those who outlive him, if they had shared any kind of inner bond at all? In recent years I had to live through so many close experiences of death, but not one person has been taken from me without my having found the tasks around me increased. The weight of this unexplained and perhaps greatest event, which only due to a misunderstanding has gained the reputation of being arbitrary and cruel, presses us (I think increasingly) more evenly and more deeply into life and places the utmost obligations on our slowly growing strengths.

I clung to these words. I did not understand what they meant, but they grounded me while I felt numb, fearful, and mute. After that winter and a long spring, when I still had not started to feel better, I saw no other possibility but to heed Rilke's advice and attach myself to pain as the path back into life. Gradually I began to understand these words—it was as much their texture and shape as their elusive meaning that encouraged me to find a way back *into* language and life. But it was a new way, charted through pain but also enriched by it, deeper and harder than any path I had taken before. And it was the only one. Moving forward meant moving with and *through* the pain rather than overcoming it, which would have meant also forgetting my father and how losing him had taught me things about myself I could not learn when he was alive. Rilke's words did not provide the consolation that all would be well again. But the repeated reading of these letters made me realize that death does not exceed our strength: "It is the highest mark etched at the vessel's rim: We are *full* whenever we reach it, and being full means (for us) a feeling of heaviness, that something is difficult ... that is all."

This collection of Rilke's letters of condolence, gathered here from numerous far-flung editions and archives for the first time, may guide other readers in finding their way back from mourning and pain into a transformed life. Rilke often finds startlingly concrete and accessible ways of describing how pain invades us. Occasionally he hews close to conventional expressions, but when he uses existing formulations, he always modifies them slightly. Thus he speaks of the "deepest" (instead, as one would expect, of the "highest") price we may have to pay to learn of our own strength; he remarks that loss requires a full "accounting" (in the literal sense of bookkeeping) of suffering, that someone died "into his own heart"; that time "assigns things to their proper place" (in the concrete sense of organizing a cupboard or room); or that he longs for objects "pulsing with the past." Where possible, I have echoed these modifications and deliberate distortions of idiomatic German (and French, in the case of two letters) to preserve the vivid tone of Rilke's letters, and their directness and sense of urgency. Rilke's original German is more studded with dashes, hyphens, ellipses, and near-stuttering repetitions than a solid English sentence (even after Dickinson) can bear. The overall impression is of a poet for whom language is a living, breathing thing, rather than a tool with which to cast polished pearls of wisdom on a page.

In all of his work, Rilke affirms our earthly life without embellishment and with the acceptance of loss as well as the great ecstasies of love. All too often, we are distracted, prejudiced, or casual in our perception of the world. Rilke encourages us to become aware of how much in the world and in our lives we yet have to even notice, and reminds us that human life should be seen as the tremendous opportunity afforded to us to understand ourselves better. The notion of a "beyond," as powerful as it may be to some, especially through religious texts on overcoming grief, provides no consolation for Rilke since it makes the deceased less approachable, and also makes us less real to ourselves. We live in the here and now after all, and any longing for another realm simply distracts us from this fact.

Not every letter in this selection from Rilke's correspondence directly concerns a death of a beloved person. He also addresses with great tact and sensitivity the painful dissolution of a deep and loving friendship and even, in a touching letter to his erstwhile lover Lou Andreas-Salomé, the loss of a beloved pet. Other letters try to diminish our terrible dread of extinction by making clearer that death may be the side of life that is turned away from us, but that it completes our existence into the fullness of being.

Shortly before his own death of leukemia in 1926 at the age of fifty-one, Rilke despaired that he had not succeeded, in spite of the monumental achievements of his poetry and the letters which proved so vitally important for so many, in finding a way to face death with equanimity. Nevertheless, he had used his abhorrence of the idea of extinction as fuel for transformation and deeper understanding. From the published recollections of his longtime confidante

Nanny Wunderly-Volkart, a woman of rare sensitivity, we know that Rilke suffered greatly during his final weeks. But he left us a cache of the most profound and extraordinary writings about death, which reach beyond his own existence to touch, inspire, and perhaps provide aid.

The book concludes with Rilke's letter to his Polish translator, in which Rilke explains how to understand the interplay of death and life, of give and take, as the totality of everything that may be experienced by us. Our task here on earth is to truly and fully experience our existence with our senses, and to transform these sensory perceptions in the deepest layers of our inner being. Then mute feeling can become expression; then pain can be imparted to ourselves and others, and lead back to life. Then, in a case as rare as Rilke's, a reflection on the inescapable reality of our death can become poetry. The loved ones whom we have lost are included in this task of transforming our experiences deep within us. It is our mission to recall our shared life with them in what Rilke calls "the invisible," by which he means that mysterious realm of spirit, memory, and intention that guides our purpose and our actions among the living.

CONTENTS

To Mimi Romanelli

———

Mimi Romanelli (1877–1970), the younger sister of the Italian art dealer and archaeologist Pietro Romanelli, was known for her beauty and musical talent. Rilke stayed in her family's small hotel in Venice in 1907. They had a romantic relationship and maintained a long correspondence.

SUNDAY, DECEMBER 8, 1907
Oberneuland near Bremen (Germany)

There is death in life, and it astonishes me that we pretend to ignore this: death, whose unforgiving presence we experience with each change we survive because we must learn to die slowly. We must learn to die: That is all of life. To prepare gradually the masterpiece of a proud and supreme death, of a death where chance plays no part, of a well-made, beatific, and enthusiastic death of the kind the saints knew to shape. Of a long-ripened death that effaces its hateful name and is nothing but a gesture that returns those laws to the anonymous universe which have been recognized and rescued over the course of an intensely accomplished life. It is this idea of death which has developed inside of me since childhood from one painful experience to the next, and which compels me to humbly endure the small death, so that I may become worthy of the one which wants us to be great.

I am not ashamed, my dear, to have cried on a recent early Sunday morning in a cold gondola as it was gliding around endless corners through parts of Venice so vaguely visible that they seemed to extend into another city far away. The voice of the *barcaiolo* who called out to be granted passage at the corner of a canal received no answer, as in the face of death.

And the bells that I had heard in my room only moments before (my room where I have lived a whole life, where I was born and where I am preparing to die) seemed so clear to me; those same bells trailed their sounds like rags behind them over the swirling waters, only to reconnect without recognition.

It is still this death which continues inside of me, which works in me, which transforms my heart, which deepens the red of my blood, which bears down heavily on the life that had been ours so that this death becomes a bittersweet drop coursing through my veins and permeating everything, and which ought to be mine forever.

And while I am completely engulfed in my sadness, I am happy to sense that you exist, beautiful one. I am happy to have flung myself without fear into your beauty just as a bird flings itself into space. I am happy, dear, to have walked with steady faith on the waters of our uncertainty all the way to that island which is your heart and where pain blossoms. Finally: happy.

To Countess Lili Kanitz-Menar

Lili Kanitz-Menar (1869–1943) was the great-niece of Rilke's acquaintance Countess Luise Schwerin (1846–1906) in whose memory he wrote the poem "Experience of Death" (1907). She performed as a concert singer and conductor under the name Lili Menar.

July 16, 1908 (evening)
Paris, 17, rue Campagne-Première

I thank you, my dear friend, for having written to me. Fifty times I've wanted to respond since receiving your letter, but couldn't get to it. There is so much that I need to get through right now: I mean in my work, and I don't have quite as much energy as I ought to. And then, to add to all of this, this incommensurate event. What is one supposed to say? How should one account for it? It is always the same question. Over the past few years, I have had to ask myself this question several times. The death of Countess Schwerin and my father's death (each of which provided me with an experience of infinite greatness and magnanimity) have resulted in the fact that I no longer fear this question. And yet it is difficult to have to face it again so closely, even in the brightest day. And in this most recent case, it is complicated by so many things: Who was this woman who lived for other people and yet, beneath everything and without knowing or admitting to it, harbored the demands of an entire life within her as if they had been left there entirely touched, so that one could often get the idea that she was also the opposite of what she wanted to be, and that both of these states would be equally true and equally unreal? And finally, what sort of relationship did one have with her, in which fondness and even admiration was so oddly compatible with resistance, rejection, and harsh judgments that one never dared to fully take stock of it and arrive at a net total? And for quite some time I experienced the kindness she displayed toward me and which eventually turned into a friendship—I don't know when—rather as a beautifully executed legacy from the wonderful sister who preceded her, than as an actual gift from her. In trying to make sense of this, I only move further away from any insight into this person. Today, my attitude toward death is that it frightens me more in those whom I failed to truly encounter and who remained inexplicable or disastrous to me, than it does in those whom I loved with certainty when they were alive, even if they burst only for a brief moment into the radiant transfiguration of intimacy which love can reach. If people took some simple pleasure in reality (which is entirely independent of time), they would never have needed to come up with the idea that they could ever again lose anything with which they had truly bonded. No constellation is as steadfast, no accomplishment as irrevocable as a connection between human beings which, at the very moment it becomes visible, works more forcefully in those invisible depths where our existence is as lasting as gold lodged in stone, more constant than a star.

This is why I agree with you, my dear friend, when you say that you mourn those "who go away." Alas, only those can go away from us whom we never possessed. And we cannot even grieve the fact of never really having possessed this one or that one: We would have neither time nor strength nor justification for doing so. For already the most fleeting experience of true possession (or of having something in common with another person, which is after all only double possession) flings us back into ourselves with such enormous force and requires so much of us to do there, and demands such extremely solitary development, that it would be enough to keep all of us occupied individually forever.

Is that not the case?

The letter before your last one conveyed such good news that I now wish a thousand times that your current travels and your inner resolve will very soon lead to more such news, and that you will not be remiss in sending them to me. Clara is busy at work and produces beautiful things. I will see her at the end of the week.

Your loyally devoted friend
RMRilke

To Elisabeth Freiin Schenk
zu Schweinsberg

—

Schenk zu Schweinsberg (1886–1955) was a German painter.
Rilke met her during a stay on Capri in 1908 at the house of
her aunt Alice Faehndrich, who died that same year.

SEPTEMBER 23, 1908
Paris, 77, rue de Varenne

Dear Miss von Schenk,

You've done a good deed to receive my unduly late letter without reproach and as a matter of course, just in the manner I had hoped to write to you for quite some time. Although your insight and fairness are so generous that you do not consider me obligated to respond, my joy at receiving your letter this morning was so great that I would have to quarry fifteen minutes out of even the most compressed time to compose a brief and grateful response, like a small and inconspicuous stone set into the ring of thoughts that have gathered around your news.

It is quite after my own heart that you are sending

good news from a steady inner core, which seeks to preserve its position and strength in the face of everything. What you say about your honorable aunt's passing is in line with my own feeling: that we do not have to be sad for *her*. But as to the influence of the death of someone near on those he leaves behind, it has long seemed to me that this ought to be no other than a higher responsibility. Does the person who passes away not leave all the things he had begun in hundreds of ways to be continued by those who outlive him, if they had shared any kind of inner bond at all? In recent years I had to live through so many close experiences of death, but not one person has been taken from me without my having found the tasks around me increased. The weight of this unexplained and perhaps greatest event, which only due to a misunderstanding has gained the reputation of being arbitrary and cruel, presses us (I think increasingly) more evenly and more deeply into life and places the utmost obligations on our slowly growing strengths.

You gave such a sweet turn to my personal melancholy memories with the glimpse of the small childhood picture, which I have studied quite attentively. I am sending it back to you already since nobody likes to think of such objects to be out of the home and in transit.

How much childhood is in that picture, and how everything is already settled there in the quiet, so indescribably lonely state of being a child, at the time when seated in an armchair one cannot touch the floor and with immense courage just keeps sitting there in that vast space which begins all around one and goes on and on. It is a very sweet and meaningful small picture. Thank you for letting me see it.

Continue to believe that with your feeling and with your work you take part in what is *greatest*. The more strongly you cultivate this belief inside of you, the more it will give rise to reality and world.

With the most loyal devotion,

Yours,
RMRilke

TO SIDONIE NÁDHERNÁ VON BORUTÍN

Nádherná von Borutín (1885–1950) was the host of a well-known salon and the partner of the Viennese writer and journalist Karl Kraus. She first met Rilke in 1906 and maintained a long friendship and correspondence with him. Her brother Johannes Nádherný von Borutín (1884–1913) committed suicide.

AUGUST 1, 1913
Currently Baltic Sea Spa, Heiligendamm, Mecklenburg
Grand Hôtel

My dear Sidie,

Your letter really touches my heart. On the one hand, I want to encourage you in your pain so that you will completely experience it in all its fullness, because as the experience of a new intensity it is a great *life* experience and leads everything back again to life, like everything that reaches a certain degree of greatest strength. But on the other hand, I am very concerned when I imagine how strangled and cut off you currently live, afraid of touching anything that is filled with memories (and what is not filled with memories?). You will freeze in place if you remain this way. You must not, dear. You have to move. You have to return to his things. You have to touch with your hands his things, which through their manifold relations and affinity are after all also yours. You must, Sidie (this is the task that this incomprehensible fate imposes upon you), you *must* continue his life *inside* of yours insofar as it was unfinished; his life has now passed onto yours. You, who quite truly knew him, can quite truly continue in his spirit and on his path. Make it the task of your mourning to explore what he had expected of you, had hoped for you, had wished to happen to you. If I could just convince you, my dear friend, that his influence has not vanished from your existence (how much more reliably I feel my father to be effective and helpful in me since he no longer dwells among us). Just think how much in our daily lives misleads and troubles us, and renders another person's love imprecise for us. But now he is definitely here, now he is completely free to be here and we are completely free to feel him . . . Haven't you felt your father's influence and compassion a thousand times from the universe where all, truly all, Sidie, is beyond loss? Don't believe that something that belongs to our pure realities could drop away and simply cease. Whatever had such steady influence on us had already been a reality independent of all the circumstances familiar to us here. This is precisely why we experienced it as something so different and independent of an actual need: Because from the very beginning, it had no longer been aimed at and determined by our existence here. All of our true relationships, all of our enduring experiences touch upon and pass through *everything,* Sidie, through life and death. *We must live in both, be intimately at home in both.* I know individuals who already face both the one and the other without fear and with the same love—for is life really more demystified and safely entrusted to us than that other condition? Are not both conditions in a place namelessly beyond us, out of reach? We are true and pure only in our willingness to be part of the whole, the undecided, the great, the greatest. Alas, if I could tell you just *how* I know it, then deep within your mourning, a tiny kernel of dark joy would take shape. Make it your ambition to take heart. Start doing so this very evening by playing Beethoven; he also was committed to the whole.

Yours,
Rainer

Please give my very best to Charlie.

TO ILSE ERDMANN

Between 1913 and 1922, Erdmann (1879–1924) corresponded with Rilke about his work and various challenges in her life. Rilke responded in twenty letters, which are thought to have prevented her from attempting suicide. The two met in the summer of 1917, in Munich. This letter refers to the death of Erdmann's nephew, which she experienced like the death of her own child.

SATURDAY, OCTOBER 9, 1915

[...]

What I really would like to hear much more about at the right time is that knot of coincidences which, as you suggest, is actually what keeps you confined in bodily pain. Is it possible to say more about this? I may be able to aid your response by venturing a guess. I suspect that similar experiences have also gotten me entangled in my bodily condition, which in general seems incredibly difficult to me in its duality of thing and me. In my case, there is the additional fact that although I have not had any extreme experiences of bodily pain, I've been extremely sensitive to suffering from an early age. I tend to think of physical pain as so utterly senseless that as soon as it appears, my soul yields to it as if the pain simply pushed it out of the space it usually occupies. I cannot abide pain as anything but at most an experience of intensity, and as something that teaches us what intensity can be long before we encounter it again for an instant in joy, in ecstasy, or during a period of very focused work. I would like to think that very young children pass through incredible intensities of joy, pain, and sleep, and that there are later periods when physical suffering basically remains the only example of intensity for us, because life otherwise mostly leads us to distraction.

In the process of dying, however, physical pain must often be a nasty irritation since it is surely our most present and immediate experience and thus, so to speak, not valid in relation to the general realm toward which the dying person directs himself. Pain's stubborn emphasis of a specific location forces us to become one-sided and probably contradicts the dying person's inclination to try to become part of the world more broadly. Of course this will still be accomplished entirely by present means, but to make these earthly means our own, to achieve a kind of completion in our relationships with the earth, and to inexpressibly, indescribably, breathlessly exist in the here and now: Wouldn't this be the only option for us to finally be included in more than only our earthly existence? I think we have to experience boundlessness through our incapacity to measure even the measurable. That is why Kierkegaard includes us in the seriousness of death, without attributing to us a time limit or an eternal future beyond it. To understand and passionately exhaust our physical presence on earth as one side of being in itself would be the demand placed by death on us while life, where one simply recognizes it as real, is everywhere all of life.

I remember Rodin's exasperation when Francis Jammes repeated Van Tieghem's claim that the seeds of certain flowers had arrived on earth from other stars, trapped inside meteorites. Rodin knew how much we have yet to accomplish here (indeed, what not?!) and very decidedly did not want our curiosity turned beyond and away from what is here. And yet even that is possible: to have the starred skies closely wrapped around one's heart. This is how you experienced it, I think, during those recent evening walks across the meadows when you recalled what you had learned earlier about the stars. I would have liked to have been with you then, to look up next to you and to learn something. What period of your childhood may that have been when someone recited to you the names of the stars—who? I realize that I know very little of your childhood. Almost nothing.

RMR

To Adelheid Franziska von der Marwitz

—

Adelheid Franziska von der Marwitz (1894–1944) was the sister of the German poet Bernhard von der Marwitz (1890–1918) who died during World War I and had maintained a correspondence with Rilke. Her brother's frequent recitations of Rilke's poetry introduced her to the literary culture of her time. A dedication in a book that he gave to his sister before his death quotes a poem from Rilke's The Book of Images *(1902).*

JANUARY 14, 1919
Munich, Ainmillerstrasse 34/IV

My dear and honored Miss:

Only illness could excuse a silence of the kind that I have now observed against you for months—and I would like to assure you that I am ill, if I think how much any sort of communication exceeds my strengths even with people toward whom I feel as much of a motivation and motive to write such as you. While speaking, I occasionally still get over the inhibitions that invaded my most immediate nature during the devastation of these horrific years. When actually facing another human being, I gather myself for his sake (perhaps drawing a bit on *his* strength), but when I am supposed to approach someone with my pen, I grow tired as if in deep sand. And yet the fact that Christmas would have passed without even the smallest sign of my thoughts for you on its way, I would hardly have thought possible. And I have now also failed in this instance, for time passed with all of its external pressures and the many demands that I did not meet. But I may assure you that during the few moments of more solemn and somewhat festive contemplation that the presence of a Christmas tree always prompts in me, my recollections did not just fleetingly touch upon you but I have truly thought of you, have gathered my thoughts near you, and my thinking has—let me be precise—been able to come to rest near you. And there was a moment when I was filled with the determination that we would soon be granted an actual meeting in person where we could really speak to one another, which would allow me to make up for the sin of my silence.

I ultimately did not live in the rooms with the expansive park views that your brother had intended for me to inhabit in a vivid gesture of true friendship. But it is

nonetheless not at all strange for me to think of Friedersdorf, which somehow has become familiar through my
young and dear friend's desire to host me there sometime.
I'd like to imagine that I do not need to guess but that I
can rely on a feeling of unerring certainty in thinking of
the house to which I am now all the more demonstrably
connected by the strength of his beautiful and beautifully
chosen endowment. I have to assume that all of my be-
longings in Paris have been lost but now, since I have a
few rooms of my own here, a new collection of books is
gradually starting to grow. Among its most supreme
foundations is the beautiful edition of the "Odes" (by
[Paul] Claudel). It connects me to things I have had to
forgo forever but that are also unspeakably impossible to
lose by nature: to the friend who gives himself again and
again through these books, and to Paris which remains so
intricately transformative in my life.

Whether [the poet Emile] Verhaeren was one of the
authors whom Bernhard von Marwitz especially admired, and whether he read to you from his books during
the evenings in Friedersdorf? This great poet who was so
gruesomely killed during the war at the Rouen train sta-
tion was also a wonderful and great friend to me. I will
tell you about him one day, how he was able to increasingly direct all of the force and effort that human beings

apply to God back to those *humans* in whom he had such faith, expectation, and radiant joy. In fact, he thought of redirecting in this way the faith of a great and powerful believer. He was such an insurmountable friend precisely because of this direct and radiant faith in human beings. He suspected that every person could be capable of being the most pure and most magnificent, and he was blissfully willing to do nothing so much as to admire. I lost with him, this great man, the individual who knew how to most insistently encourage me to meet my obligations. Even though he could never read a line of my writings, he believed in them with boisterous optimism, and I knew he thought me capable of exactly *that* which would be my innermost joy to achieve. I recall all of this with particularly deep emotion since I now hold in my hands his final book, *Les Flammes hautes* [1917]. I have been reading aloud from it for the past three days almost without interruption. If you could only be here with me so I could share with you the happiness of these great poems, they would let you realize what we all now need most urgently: that transience is not separation. For we, transient as we are, have it in common with those who have left us—and they and we are at once united in one *being* in which separation is just as unthinkable. Would we otherwise be able to understand such poems, if they were only the statements of a future dead person? Don't they address—inside of us—besides the present conditions also continually something unlimited and unrecognizable? Yes, I think that the spirit cannot make itself so small that it concerns nothing but our existence in the here and now: Where it rushes toward us, we are both the living and the dead.

I realize only now to what extent the contributions I assembled for the Yearbook [an anthology edited by Rilke's publisher] all serve *this* conviction, which has been confirmed for me via "Experience" [a prose piece by Rilke], recounted as precisely as possible, and to which I also allude in the grotesque poem "Death." The person leaning against the tree became, so to speak, the more expressive marker of the scale calibrating between life and death. It is an image I cannot use without remembering how Romain Rolland once played for me a small musical fragment which came (he assured me) from antiquity and that was nothing but a gravestone inscription in notes. Before I knew back then *what* this music was meant to express, I described to him that it gave me the sensation of the movement of two pans of a single scale quietly settling into equilibrium, and I nearly shuddered with joy when he confessed that it was an epitaphium that had been found carved on a stele dating to the fifth century before Christ. But the peculiar "Experience" of the person leaning into the tree, which is hard to describe, means to me—I almost want to say—the natural induction into an even deeper and more invisibly grasped balance, for which the image of a scale is no longer needed. This gentle, mere presence of a human being, of someone alive, on the side of death is like the magical situation in that Greek poem where two lovers trade outfits and join in an embrace, now confused and confounded in each other's clothing and warmth. It constitutes a quiet and loving exchange of what is external, while the blissful hesitation of the modulation is close to becoming purest certainty.

The poem "Death" finally conjures up the moment when (while I was standing one night on the beautiful bridge in Toledo) a shooting star which fell through outer space in a taut and slow curve passed at the same time (how shall I put this?) through inner space: The dividing contour of the body was no longer there. And just as sight had done in this case, at an earlier time my hearing had announced to me this unity: Once on Capri, while I was standing under the olive trees in the garden one night, a bird call that forced me to close my eyes was at once inside of me and outside, as if in a single, undivided space of absolute extension and clarity!

Since I have now told you all of this, may I also send you the Almanac [a sample of new writings] published by Insel? Even the beautiful poem by Countess [Anna de]

Noailles will now, with the awareness of those connections, not seem random to you. And allow me the pleasure of recommending some books to you in the future and of occasionally sending you one that I like: Verhaeren's *Flammes hautes*, for example, as soon as I receive more copies! It's still slow and complicated with French books!

Yours,
Rilke

To Lou Andreas-Salomé

The Russian-born writer Lou Andreas-Salomé (1861–1937) was the first woman to become a psychoanalyst under the supervision of Sigmund Freud. In 1897, while in an open marriage, Andreas-Salomé began a romantic relationship of several years with Rilke. She introduced him to Russia and mentored his career as a poet. They remained friends and corresponded until Rilke's death; Rilke wrote his last letter to her. Her dog Drushok died in 1919.

JANUARY 21, 1919
Munich, 34 Ainmillerstrasse, IV

My dear Lou,

I owe it to several peculiarly and irrefutably urgent circumstances, in spite of my difficulties with writing, that in this hour of death it has been possible for me to be with you in more tangible ways. (Among them a visit to the Fürstenhäuser guesthouse, which I entered for the first time since—"back then.")

Your letter recalled to my heart the depth of your devotion to your little friend. You are now living through days of suffering, and yet I know that you especially will experience these moments as a specific way of growing more familiar and closer.

To account for the duration of one of these small heart-star's orbits is, of course, also an initiation into one's own life, and even though these cheerful moons reflect the purest world-sun for us, perhaps it was their always averted side through which we were related to the infinite life-realm beyond.—

Wonderful that you have worked so much and with such youthful joy: eight books safely in the vault!—

I have made a commitment to sit at home and see nobody (with the possible exception of [Rudolf] Kassner and two or three others). A good time to ask you for *"Rodinka"* [Andreas-Salomé's memoir of her childhood]; I hesitate only because I wonder whether I'd rather have you read it to me (as you did for Ilse)? There have been so many times already where it has become urgent that we see one another, and then each time the moment passed because I was so weighed down by all sorts of inhibitions. You are not by chance thinking of visiting Munich?

You probably know the Ainmillerstrasse, if you have ever visited the old [author Eduard von] Keyserling (I can't remember whether that had actually happened). It is a side street off Leopoldstrasse, the third one to the left, after you've passed Georgen- and Franz-Josef-Strasse. The view from my room (which is an artist's studio) is over rooftops, and in the distance rises the tower and dome of the Church of St. Ursula. Just before dusk it often looks a bit Italian, like those inlays made of pieces of marble which travelers used to bring back from Florence in the past.

I did not see [the author] Ellen Delp very much and then only with instinctual caution. She lives, I think, from believing that things will "just work out," and in this way she cannot be entirely true.

Thank you, Lou; this brief epistolary get-together has done me a lot of good, on the inside.

Rainer

TO ADELHEID VON DER MARWITZ

(See letter dated January 14, 1919.)

SEPTEMBER 11, 1919
Soglio (Bergell, Graubünden)

My dear young friend:

The joy brought by your letter has many sides: Let me recount at least a few. First, this is what we welcome now above all, that human beings are making a new start here and there to rebuild life with the strength and the faith of their indestructible hearts. There are others who could try this but who still just stand there, staring and trying to make sense of it all, and for whom sadness and sloth finally become utterly insurmountable. And this even though, based on feeling and reflection, only one thing is urgently needed: to attach oneself somewhere to nature with unconditional purpose, to what is strong, striving, and bright, and to move forward without guile, even if it can happen only in the least important, daily matters.

Each time we tackle something with joy, each time we open our eyes toward a yet untouched distance, we transform not only this and the next moment, but we also rearrange and gradually absorb the past inside of us. We dissolve the foreign body of pain of which we know neither its actual consistency and makeup nor how many (perhaps) life-affirming stimuli it imparts, once it has been dissolved, to our blood!

Death, especially the most completely felt and experienced death, has never remained an obstacle to life for a surviving individual, because its innermost essence is not contrary to us (as one may occasionally suspect), but it is more knowing about life than we are in our most vital moments. I always think that such a great weight, with its tremendous pressure, somehow has the task of forcing us into a deeper, more intimate layer of life so that we may grow out of it all the more vibrant and fertile. I gained this experience very early on through various circumstances, and it was then confirmed from pain to pain: What is here and now is, after all, what has been given and is expected of us, and we must attempt to transform everything that happens to us into a new familiarity and friendliness with it. For where else should we direct our senses, which after all have been exquisitely designed to grasp and master what is here? And how may we evade the duty to admire what God has entrusted to us, for this surely prepares us completely for all future and eternal admiration! So, when I understood your cheerful and lively words in this sense and with utmost agreement, it increased my joy to such a degree that I thought to recognize you in it quite clearly: Somehow I had long suspected that such a decisive leap would come from you. There it was—and I now feel a kind of pride and satisfaction in having guessed and anticipated quite correctly from your earlier letters what you are capable of. You have been able to establish yourself anew in a place that had become familiar during many years of your childhood and youth. That you feel blessed again in that place to tackle new tasks and desired projects, and that the warmth of accomplishing something each day lets you experience a new degree of feeling alive: This is so much that there is nothing left for your friend to wish for besides hoping that everything may remain exactly like this. Your youth, your untainted will, and the heartfelt and natural direction of the path you've so courageously chosen all vouch for the likelihood that this will be the case. The fact that you could make the effort to engage fully in the activities of people your age who share your aspirations is a sign of the most noble and admirable courage, and you are experiencing already how these efforts are paying off on the inside.—What you told me gave me an idea of the affection of your small and harmonious yet vibrant circle, and I would like for you to return their expression of sympathy. I would be delighted to contribute an hour to your gatherings by giving a bit of myself and receiving from all of you in turn, and to share in your joy and happiness!

I have not yet been able to get back to working productively. There is no one but me to chastise and reproach myself for not yet being far enough along to grow some new vines and spread a few leaves over the ruination of the past few years. Perhaps they are pushing through somewhere, but the surface is only rubble and desolation, with no new growth in sight. I ought to begin in any random spot, right now, today, immediately, but it's not a matter of my being picky when, in spite of this realization, I am waiting for certain conditions which I expect to provide a kind of specific support. I am hoping for a small, old house and an old garden where I may spend a long period by myself with nothing but nature and a few things pulsing with the gentle rhythms of the past. Without this kind of support, I do not think I will be able to muster the concentration that would reveal to me the quietest, most guarded spot of my inner nature where new sources well up. I have already talked with your brother Banni of this need, which he understands completely and wholeheartedly!

Now it's a matter of finding out whether something

like this exists somewhere. It almost came to pass here, if only on a provisional basis. I've taken up residence in this tiny mountain spot (barely an hour from the Italian border) in an ancient Palazzo named Salis, which has managed to hold on to its ancestral furnishings and an old garden edged by trimmed boxwood, even though decades ago all of it was turned into a hotel. To top it off, they have granted me access to the Count's old library (otherwise off-limits for guests) with a room perfectly after my personal taste that reminds me of earlier arrangements where I had been most comfortable. Take good care of yourself. I will remain in Switzerland as long as it remains feasible, at this address—please write to me again.

In friendship,

Rilke

To Anita Forrer

Anita Forrer (1901–1996) was a Swiss graphologist. In 1919, she wrote to Rilke after she had seen him at a public reading. The "question" in this letter refers to Forrer's query whether her somewhat older, female friend had understood the intimate nature of an encounter while Forrer was still innocent of such knowledge. Her family had sent Forrer to a therapist to break off the relationship. Rilke and Forrer exchanged a series of letters from 1920 until 1926, but met only once in person at the home of Nanny Wunderly-Volkart in 1923.

FEBRUARY 14, 1920
Locarno (Tessin)
Pension Villa Muralto

Dear Anita,

Between half-packed suitcases and lots of distractions from friends visiting from near and far, I have left your two letters still without the kind of heartfelt response that I feel for each of the ones you send to me. I will tell you right away, Anita, that I have forgotten *nothing*. Your question to your friend, along with all the rest of your confusion, can definitely be blamed on that "educator." It was, of course, what people call "a bit coarse," this question, but the doctor's intrusive actions were equally so. Here you have simply *passed* something *along* which was alien to you as well. You have to consider what kind of confusion and turmoil his explanations prompted in you, and so it was not much of a stretch to ask the beloved friend: Did you *deliberately* cause this disaster for me? The fact that your friendship broke up over this question, at least for the time being, was probably inevitable. For once this lingering suspicion had been introduced, all the conditions that can make a love unsuspecting and joyful had been suspended. Perhaps this loss is not as definitive as you think right now; perhaps one day your friend will understand the plight which caused you to ask this question—perhaps only a pause has occurred between you: One must let life run its course. The human being destroys so many things on his own, and it is not in his power to restore anything. Nature, by contrast, has all the power to heal as long one does not eavesdrop or interrupt it.

It also makes me happy, Anita, that you have understood me. If only I had been able to take away this ghost of a burden from you earlier, since it is a shame for each of your young days that suffered through it. But now you are remaking everything for yourself with your cheerful confidence. Both of your letters confirm to me your renewal for which, by the way, I ought not take credit: Since it was you who wrote to me first, it had basically already occurred. All you needed was to speak with someone for a bit, dear child, to claim an inner property which had been entirely prepared in silence all along. What could I contribute to this, what would I ever be able to add to this? I could only *show* you what you had already obtained inside yourself. It still seems to me the most wonderful thing in life that the blunt and rough nature of any intrusion and even an obvious disturbance can become the occasion to create a new order within ourselves. It is the most splendid achievement of our life force that it finds a way of looking at evil as something good and fundamentally reverses it. Without this kind of alchemy we would all be evil, for everyone is touched and invaded by evil, and anyone could be caught at a given moment in being "bad." Not to stay put in that place but *to live, that* is the secret. Nothing is more untenable than what is bad. No human being should ever think that he "is" bad; he only has to move ever so slightly, and instantly he isn't bad anymore.

Once I stood on a bridge in Paris and glimpsed from afar on a brick road leading down to the river a suicide victim, wrapped in an oilcloth, who had just been pulled from the Seine. Suddenly I heard someone next to me say something. It was a young blond carriage driver in a blue jacket, very young indeed, strawberry-blond, with an intelligent, cleverly pointed face. He had a wart on his chin sprouting a stiff bunch of red hairs almost cheekily, like a paintbrush. When I turned toward him, he gestured with his head toward the object that held both of our attention and said with a wink: *"Dites donc, celui-là, s'il a pu encore faire ça, il aurait bien pu faire autre chose"* ["So, tell me, this one, if he could still do that, he could have done something else"].

I watched him, a bit astonished, as he was already walking back to his enormous cart heaped with rocks, for truly: *What* shouldn't a person be able to achieve with precisely the kind of force that is needed to dissolve the powerful, tremendous attachments of life! From that moment on I have known with certainty that the worst things, and even despair, are only a kind of abundance and an onslaught of existence that one decision of the heart could turn into its opposite. Where things become truly difficult and unbearable, we find ourselves in a place already very close to its transformation. Farewell for today, Anita.

Rainer

To Erwein Freiherr von Aretin

Von Aretin (1887–1952) was a German astronomer, jour-
nalist, editor, and author. Rilke met him in Munich in 1915,
after which they maintained a long correspondence touch-
ing on subjects including astronomy and scientific discov-
eries. This letter refers to the death of his father, Anton
Freiherr von Aretin.

May 1, 1921
Castle Berg am Irchel
Canton Zurich, Switzerland

My dear friend,

Your most recent letter prepared me for how close you
have been living to that great and nearest loss, which the
announcement of last night now makes real to me.

I would like to be with you in response as quickly as
possible with a few lines.

I am certain that you are filled with emotion yet com-
posed, and under the influence of the pure and quiet laws
which, given our limitations, can be nothing but mute and
ruthless.

Your mother will find in her faith that deepest consolation which originates in the very center of pain. May all of you feel able to make her condition of having been left behind gentle and forgiving.

It is otherwise indeed our grief's peculiar prerogative that on *those* occasions when it does not seem disturbed by the contradiction that we sometimes think of a life as apparently unfinished, interrupted, torn off, it is allowed to be a true act of learning, a true accomplishment, the purest, most consummate coming to our senses. And this coming to our senses is nowhere greater than in the unique task imposed on us when the loss of the father at his advanced age impacts us: It obliges us, in a way, to compose ourselves anew and to employ our inner capacities independently for the first time.

As long as our father is alive, we are after all a kind of relief set against him (hence the tragic dimension of the conflicts). It is only this blow that turns us into completely rounded figures, free and, alas, freestanding on all sides . . . (the mother, always courageous, has placed us from the beginning as far outside as she could—).

Only this, dear friend, by warmly extending my hands to you and thinking of you and yours.

Always yours,
Rilke

To Nanny Wunderly-Volkart

Nanny Wunderly-Volkart (1878–1962) was the wife of the Swiss industrialist Hans Wunderly. During the last years of Rilke's life, after he had lost his citizenship when the Austro-Hungarian Empire ended after World War I, Rilke lived in Switzerland at the Château de Muzot (a small stone manor) which was first rented and then purchased for him by Wunderly's cousin Werner Reinhart. Rilke and Wunderly-Volkart, whom he called Nike, maintained a long friendship and correspondence.

June 2, 1921
Etoy

[…]

The small news clipping that I have enclosed from the *Figaro* (entitled *"L'autobus—char d'assaut"* ["The passenger bus—tank"]): May I get it back at some point? I have re-read it again and again, even though it contains only one of the infinite number of miscellaneous items that are reported each day by the dozen; (the *Neue Zürcher Zeitung* [newspaper] puts them always in one section, "Misfortunes and Crimes"; are misfortunes the crimes of fate?).

Poor little Lucie Ramé from Essonnes, who is already unlucky enough to tap away all day behind a window on a typewriter, now a bus drives into that window and crushes her chest over the small heart … dear God: *What for?* Similar things have been reported hundreds and hundreds of times, but suddenly it's no longer bearable! All of contemporary life (including "nonbelievers") agrees perhaps only on one thing, which is not to draw any final conclusions from the death of Miss Lucie Ramé, although, to be precise, no news item can counter it. It means either: Death is such an indescribable, immeasurable value that God allows it to be inflicted on us at any time even in the most senseless manner, simply because he may not bestow anything greater on us. Or this news item can be read *in this way:* Our personal existence has no significance for God, and far from assigning it its duration, he knows nothing of its presence and of the unbelievable value we attribute to how long it may last. If this insight were experienced *truly* just once, it would certainly not cause the damage in freer minds that God would be denied; but it could succeed in demarcating the essential conditions of his existence against those of our own. Nothing makes us more incapable of truly experiencing God than our stubbornness in wanting to recognize his hand *in those places* where it has always been withheld. By imagining his involvement in so many things that matter to us, we probably overlook its signs and most glaring proofs as they become manifest elsewhere. So much of the sorrow which the war inflicted on me still resulted from my incapacity to reconcile the perishing of so many talented and indeed extremely distinguished individuals with God! We all carry in our blood some kind of misunderstanding of God's "protection," which cheats us of the freedom that belongs to us and whose first consequence (if we knew how to use it) would be a different relationship to death.

The distance between birth and death above which we write "I" is not a measure for God; life & death constitute for him probably only a small degree of separation, and perhaps a continual series of lives and deaths is needed for God to have the impression: one. Perhaps only all of creation in its totality is permitted to call itself "I" before him, and all the fluctuations of appearing and vanishing *inside* it would then be its own concern.

It is a shame that God did not know little Lucie Ramé; there is no way of letting him know that the bus crushed her to death—for even that bus, the *"char d'assaut,"* he never caught a glimpse of! We have to get used to the fact that we rest in the pause between two of God's breaths: for that means: to be in time. It is conceivable that he was linked to creation only via the act through which he externalized it out of himself. In that case, only that which has not been created would have a right to think of itself as continually attached to God. The brief time of our existence is probably precisely the period when we lose all connection to him and, drifting apart from him, become enmeshed in the creation *which he leaves alone.* We can rely only on memories and premonitions, for there is surely an even more urgent task of applying our senses to what is present here and to expand them so much that they converge into a single sense of awe and admiration.—

[…]

To Reinhold von Walter

The writer and translator Reinhold von Walter (1882–1965) maintained a correspondence with Rilke between 1907 and 1921.

June 4, 1921
Le Prieuré, Etoy
Canton de Vaud, Suisse

[…]

Whether I have made any progress in the kind of confidence and trust in death of which you write to me will also only become clear within that great work [of the *Duino Elegies* (1922)]. You are correct: We have been tasked with nothing as unconditionally as learning on a daily basis how to die. But our knowledge of death is enriched not by the refusal of life. It is only the ripe fruit of the here and now, when seized and bitten into, that spreads its indescribable flavor in us.

[…]

Yours,
R. Maria

To Mrs. Gertrud Ouckama Knoop

—

Gertrud Ouckama Knoop (1869–1967) was the wife of
Rilke's friend Gerhard Ouckama Knoop and the mother of
Vera, a dancer and childhood friend of Rilke's daughter,
Ruth. In 1919, Vera died of leukemia after a long illness at
age nineteen. Rilke resumed his correspondence with the
bereaved mother only in 1921, who then sent him her
daughter's unedited diary of her last years. The letter was
written in response to receiving this chronicle. Rilke's
Sonnets to Orpheus, *written in February 1922, bear the*
subtitle "A Memorial for Vera Ouckama Knoop."

[JANUARY 4, 1922]

My dear friend,

What can I say? Just as you did not find yourself able to
add anything in your own words to the diary entries you
copied for me in your last letter, I am now just as incapable of communicating anything concerning myself to you
as long as I am still the reader of these pages, hunched
over them, always, even when I look up. I had not had the
slightest idea of any of this and did not even know any-

thing specific about the beginnings of the illness, and now your letter introduced me all at once to something that touches, deeply moves, and overwhelms me in so many ways. If one were to read your account and it concerned any young girl whom one did not know, it would already be close enough. But now this is all about Vera whose dark and strangely concentrated charms remain so unspeakably unforgettable to me that I can recall them with immense immediacy. Right now, while writing this, I would be afraid to close my eyes lest I feel her charms completely overwhelm me in my being in the here and now.

How much, how much, how very much has Vera been all of that for which these recollections of your pain offer such deep and irrevocable testimony. And—isn't it true?—how wonderful, how unique, how incomparable is a human being! There, where everything was allowed to get used up which otherwise would have had to last for the duration of a long lifetime, there (where?) now suddenly occurred this abundance of light in the girl's heart, and in it appear, in this infinite light, the two outermost edges of her pure insight: That pain is an error. That pain is a dull misunderstanding arising from our bodies which drives its stony wedge into the unity of heaven and earth—and on the other side this unified oneness of her heart open to anything, with its unity of the existing and the enduring world, this affirmation and acceptance of life, this joyful, heartfelt, and (up to the end) completely capable way of belonging with the here and now—alas, only with the here and now?! No (she could not know this in those first attacks of decay and departure!)—with the whole, with far more than the here and now. Oh, how very, very much she loved, how she reached with her heart's antennae beyond anything that could be grasped and encompassed here—during those tender floating pauses in suffering which were still granted to her, full of the dream of recovery . . .

It seems, dear friend, that fate has taken great care to lead you each time beyond its usual edge along a stony precipice of life to the gorge of death, with an ever more exposed heart. Now you live and observe and feel out of infinite experience.—

For me, my cherished friend, for me, however, it is in the form of a tremendous obligation to my innermost, most serious, and (even if I reach it only from a distance) most blissful self that I was granted possession of these pages on the first evening of a new year.

Yours,
Rilke

To Countess Alexandrine Schwerin

Alexandrine Schwerin (1880–1957) was the daughter-in-law of Countess Luise von Schwerin, who met and then invited Rilke and his wife, Clara, to stay at her country residence, Castle Friedelhausen (near Frankfurt) in the summers of 1905 and 1906. Her husband was Count Eberhard (Ebo) von Schwerin. The letter likely refers to the death of her father, Philipp Friedrich Alexander Fürst zu Eulenburg (1847–1921).

June 16, 1922
Château de Muzot sur Sierre (Valais)

My dear Countess:

Just as sometimes, when one tries two keys on an organ at once, an entire storm of sound erupts, you have allowed me over here to feel the entire sudden excess of suffering that now makes up your life! I could not write since I had visitors staying here at Muzot, one after the other, long-awaited friends—but I still cannot write now, after they have left, for what has struck you there, especially the second blow which extends so far into the future, eludes any direct expression of sympathy. Believe me, my dear Countess, that my silent and heartfelt thoughts are with you . . . And also from my heart, with Count Ebo!

Where each of us may find the sources of consolation when thus afflicted by a loss is a question of personal experience and fate. I hope that somewhere in the thicket of your sprawling pain you may come upon the small spring that has already cried all the tears before, and, indeed, *for* you in advance. For it is unthinkable that this ever possible, providential pain, which is so often aimed at and inflicted upon human beings, is *in*consolable. This pain in particular allows the most personal and sweetest consolation to come to ripen for us: The greatest, nearest, and most pressing human loss in particular shelters the fruit of consolation most reliably. Get to the bottom of this intensity and have faith in what is most horrible, instead of fighting it off—it reveals itself for those who can trust it, in spite of its overwhelming and dire appearance, as a kind of initiation. By way of loss, by way of such vast and immeasurable experiences of loss, we are quite powerfully introduced into the *whole*. Death is only a relentless way of making us familiar and even intimate with the side of our existence that is turned away from us (what should

I stress *more:* "our" or "existence"? Both carry the heaviest emphasis here, as if counterbalanced by the weight of all of the stars!).

I can write to you in this way especially since you are in Friedelhausen, where my own lengthy period of learning about these matters began with the death of your mother-in-law, Countess Schwerin. What I began to learn back then with amazement and initially with disbelief, was strongly confirmed later by the loss of my father. He had been so dear to me that for my entire childhood the mere thought that one day he could no longer exist brought all of nature, both outside and inside of me, to a standstill.—But actually, under the influence of ever deeper initiation, nature eventually became more expressive, touching and moving to me with every loss that I suffered as if it brought me ever closer to its heart.

If I were to visit Germany this summer or fall, dear little Friedelhausen would fortunately be along the way!—A thousand greetings sent with my enduring affection.

Ever at your service,
Rilke

To Elisabeth von der Heydt

———

Auguste Elisabeth von der Heydt (1864–1961) was the wife of the banker, art collector, and writer Karl von der Heydt. Rilke first met the couple in 1905, when he was invited to stay at their country estate. They became friends and patrons who maintained a long correspondence with him starting in that same year. The friendship cooled after Rilke supported the November 1918 revolution in Germany, which resulted in the end of the monarchy. The letter is written in response to the death of Karl von der Heydt and mentions the daughters, Gisela Maria (von Palm) and Gerda-Dorothea.

August 17, 1922
Château de Muzot sur Sierre/Valais, Switzerland

Dear Mrs. von der Heydt,

I am so very moved that I want to extend my hands to you: Please let me repeat in my own handwriting what I had already hastened to assure you in yesterday's telegram, for all of my hours have been under the influence of the distressing news from the instant I received word.

May you be able to feel that I am among those who were devoted to and attached to Karl von der Heydt because of his deep and quiet worth. It would be enough to grasp the nature of our relationship in this way to understand immediately that it will become most lasting based on my remembrance of him and augmented in its nature with an unspeakable amount of melancholy and awe.

Even the brief announcement of his death gave me a palpable impression of the powerful example of patience and forbearance that he presented to your eyes and heart for the last few years, and how he proved daily his just and pure endurance and ultimate courage.

I would like to think that I had not been as distant from all of that as it appears to be, given the circumstances. And yet, in spite of this tangible inner closeness, I am now overwhelmed by the self-reproach that in the recent and also more distant past I had not been more communicative with the loyal and understanding friend of so many years. My silence was partly caused by worries and concerns, which kept my pen in check because I realized that one should write to him only in a cheerful tone. I had also been quite happy to be able to prepare truly good news for him for the very near future: Soon I would have written to tell him about the completion of a great work that had lingered in uncertainty for ten long years. I waited to make this announcement only because I hoped to send him, ideally at the same time with the letter, a few selections as well. I have pictured many times that especially this new and quite slowly grown work would have been as dear and near to him as was, once upon a time, the *Book of Hours,* which was actually the true basis of his heartfelt and often helpful confidence in me which I have been so honored to acknowledge! The sudden deprivation not to count Karl von der Heydt any longer among those who will receive this book one day is one of the most sensitive areas of my pain which is otherwise nourished by such deep memories . . .

May I ask you to remind Baroness Palm and her family, and especially Gerda-Dorothea, that I feel myself included in their great affliction through the awareness of my own loss. All of you may grant me this painful right on which I also draw for the privilege, dear Frau von der Heydt, of remaining loyally yours in old friendship for the future.

Yours,
Rilke

TO MARGUERITE MASSON

*Marguerite Masson (1887–1972) was the sister of the
painter Odette Ruffy (1892–1915). Antoine Contat, vice
chancellor of Switzerland and a patron of the arts, introduced her to Rilke in 1922.*

JANUARY 4, 1923
Château de Muzot sur Sierre
Valais

Dear Madame:

After receiving your letter I was very happy that Monsieur Contat had allowed me to write to you and send the
book [*Duino Elegies*] which had been destined for you, because of what you say about your life: that its most painful
event was also the greatest. This is, basically, the secret
thesis of these pages, and it is perhaps even the innate
belief that brought them into existence—this conviction
that what is greatest about our existence and renders it
precious and ineffable also makes very careful use of our
painful experiences to enter into our soul. It is true that

sometimes also happiness may serve as a pretext to initiate us into that which, by its very nature, surpasses us. But in such cases it is much easier to understand right away that it wants only the best for us, although it is surely no less difficult *to make use* of this good we receive in the midst of happiness than it is to acknowledge that there is something positive at the bottom of the absences inflicted on us by pain. Every day when looking at these beautiful white roses, I ask myself whether they are not the most perfect image of this unity, and (I would even say) this identity of absence and presence that perhaps forms the fundamental equation of our life? The writings of Malte L. Brigge represent only a first step or two in that direction. One would have to go there much more forcefully and, above all, one would have to make it one's mission to destroy those ancient and inherited doubts that separate us from the best part of our own strengths. We distrust those strengths to the point that we let them become strange to us, because they offer or impose on us, depending on the circumstances, other ways of permanence than those we believe to be compatible with our personality. It is a blessed moment of inner life when one decides or resolves from now on to love with all one's strength and unflinchingly *that* which one fears the most, that which has made us—according to our own measure—suffer *too much*. Don't you believe that once such a decision has been made, the word "separation" is nothing but a name stripped of all meaning, unless it were the wonderful anonymity of an infinite number of discoveries, unheard-of harmonies, and unimaginable encounters . . .

I thank you, dear Madame, for this beautiful, silent photograph. It keeps the fragile memory in balance when one places enough white roses on the other side.

Yes, please do me the honor, if one day you should come to Muzot with Monsieur Contat (which I hope very much), to pay a visit to a longtime friend whom you will always find loyal and much obliged.

R. M. Rilke

To Countess Margot
Sizzo-Noris-Crouy

Sizzo-Noris-Crouy (1891–1977) translated Rilke's immensely popular prose poem "The Love and Death of Cornet Christopher Rilke" (published 1912) into French. They maintained a long correspondence. Her mother, Livia Crouy-Chanel (born in 1859), died in 1922.

Day of Epiphany [January 6], 1923
Château de Muzot sur Sierre, Valais

My dearest, honorable Countess,

Just a few days ago I reread your cheerful letter from the summer and couldn't quite understand how my pen had become so tardy as to leave your kind and so richly communicative lines unanswered for so long. And yet I did not write right away! It is as if my pen—unfortunately we use the same for all of our writing, for work and our correspondence—absolutely insisted on some rest after the great efforts of the past year . . .

And I needed rest, too! After such a great effort there

always follows a period of feeling at a loss, not as if one were actually empty but because certain reserves of one's being have been transformed, spent, and basically become forever unavailable for personal use. One doesn't want to start looking right away for other inner property—one doesn't quite know *what* one wants in this state of hesitating and gradually re-orienting oneself—and it turns out that during such periods one does not like to say "I." For what could one say about such an "I," without forcing oneself to make an effort? Often, during such moments in the past, I benefited from a change of surroundings that proved helpful both for getting rest and for starting something new. (Part of my restlessness might even be explained by the fact that each time when such a period of intensity ended, I rushed to accept *any* kind of external change as somehow helpful ...). This time it was also perhaps going to be like this. I was determined to leave Muzot, whether to move back to Paris (which would have been useful for some research I have long planned), or whether to take a trip to our ancestral home, Kärnten, which I do not yet know, and to see whether it would be possible to settle there ... The family crest, which dates back to what I think may be the fourteenth century, supposedly still exists, and may even have been regularly restored in the Assembly House in Klagenfurt. I myself, not only because I am the last male in my family, felt like the right person to complete a wide circle with a kind of homecoming there, if that is possible without using force, and to settle for some time in the place where, based on myth and written records, we originated. ("Csakathurn," which is supposed to be one of the oldest estates of the Kärnten branch of the Rilke family, is, if I am not mistaken, a hereditary fief and title in the family of Count Festetics, one of your relatives!)—But then the slightest attempt to become mobile was instantly fraught with so many difficulties that I ultimately relented and locked myself in for another winter in Muzot, with the best intentions to make also this monastic period as productive as possible. I immediately accepted several different translation projects, which will probably keep me quite busy during the quiet months. I would have made more progress already if I did not experience health problems each time I make a somewhat more strenuous effort or get excited by something, which is probably also a result of the somewhat forced efforts of my previous period of work.

All this about me, my dear, dear Countess! All of this, while your latest letter presented such an immediate and unexpectedly painful occasion to speak of you and *to you*. But especially because this is so very much needed, I wanted first to have made myself truly present to you again after such a long silence, so that the warm words of empathy which I feel so naturally compelled to address to you do not come to you from too vague a place. So that you may get a better sense of *who* speaks these words, and from what circumstances. Words ... can they be words of consolation?—I am not sure about this, and I do not quite believe that one can or should be consoled for a loss as sudden and great as the one you just suffered ...

"Woe to those who have been consoled" comes close to what the courageous Marie Lenéru wrote in her remarkable and strange "Journal," and here indeed consolation would be one of many distractions, a diversion, and thus at bottom something frivolous and unproductive. Time itself does not "console," as people say superficially; at best it assigns things to their proper place and creates an order. And even this works only because later we pay so little mind and hardly give any consideration to that order to which time so quietly contributes, that instead of admiring everything that now softened and reconciled comes to rest in the great Whole, we treat it as the forgetfulness and weakness of our heart just because our pain is no longer as acute. Alas, how little the heart *forgets*—and how strong it would be if we did not stop it from completing its tasks before they have been fully and truly accomplished!—Not wanting to be consoled for such a loss: That should be our instinct. Instead we should make it our deep and searing curiosity to explore such loss completely and to experience the particular and singular nature of *this* loss and its impact within our life. Indeed, we ought to muster the noble greed to enrich our inner world precisely with *this* loss and its significance and weight ... The more deeply we are impacted by such loss and the more violently it shakes us, the more it is our *task* to reclaim as our possession in new, different, and definitive ways that which, by virtue of being lost, is now so hopelessly emphasized. *This* would then amount to the infinite achievement of overcoming on the spot all the negative, sluggish, and indulgent dimensions that are found in every experience of pain. This is active pain that works on the inside, the only kind that has any meaning and is worthy of us. I do not love the Christian ideas of a Beyond, and I increasingly distance myself from them without, of course, thinking of attacking them. They may have their value and purpose, like so many other hypotheses about the divine periphery. But for me the danger is not only that they render those who have passed away less concrete and at least for the moment less reachable for us. But even we ourselves, in our longing for a beyond *away* from here, become in that process less concrete and less earthbound, while it is our obligation—as long as we are *here* and related to tree, flower, and soil—to remain earthbound in the purest sense, and even yet to become so! In my case what had died for me, so to speak, had died into my own heart. When I looked for the person who had passed away, he gathered *inside* of me in peculiar and such surprising ways, and it was deeply moving to feel that he now existed *only* there. My enthusiasm for serving, deepening, and honoring his existence there gained the upper hand almost at the same moment when the pain would otherwise have invaded and devastated the entire landscape of my mind. When I remember how—often with the most extreme difficulties in understanding and accepting each other—I loved my father! During my childhood, my thoughts often became confused and my heart froze at the mere thought that at some point he might cease to be; my existence seemed to me so entirely determined by him (my existence which from the beginning was aimed in such a different direction!) that to my innermost self his departure was synonymous with my own demise. But death is *so* deeply rooted in the nature of love (if we only become cognizant of death without being misled by the ugliness and suspicions attached to it) that it nowhere contradicts love. *Where to,* finally, can death drive a person we have unspeakably borne in our heart but *into* that very heart, where would the "idea" of this beloved being and his unceasing influence (for *how* could *this* influence cease, which, while he was still alive among us, had already become more and more independent of his tangible presence) … *where* would this always secret influence be more secure than *within* us?! Where can we get closer to this influence, celebrate it more purely, and submit to it better than when it appears in concert with our own voices as if our heart had learned a new language, a new song, a new strength!—I reproach all modern religions for providing their believers with consolations and embellishments of death instead of giving their soul the means to reconcile and communicate with it. With death, with its complete and unmasked cruelty: a cruelty so horrific that *it* completes the circle by reaching all the way back to an extreme mildness which is as great, pure, and utterly *clear* (all consolation is murky!) as we never imagined the sweetest spring day to be! But mankind has never even taken a first step to experience this deepest gentleness, which, if even only a few of us truly received it, could perhaps gradually permeate and make transparent all conditions of life. Nothing has been done to experience *this* most abundant and soothing gentleness—except perhaps during the most ancient and guileless periods of the past whose secrets we have nearly lost. I am certain that the content of all of the "initiations" anyone ever experienced was nothing but a "key" that allowed us to read the word "death" *without* negating it. Just like the moon, life surely has a side that is permanently turned away from us, and which is *not* its opposite but its complement to attain perfection, consummation, and the truly complete and round sphere and orb of *being*.

There should be no fear that we are not strong enough to endure any and even the closest and most horrible experience of death. Death is not *beyond* our strength, it is the highest mark etched at the vessel's rim: We are *full* whenever we reach it, and being full means (for us) a feeling of heaviness, that something is difficult . . . that is all.—I do not mean to say that one should *love* death. But one should love life so generously and without calculating and selecting that one automatically always includes it (the half turned away from life) in one's love, too. This is what actually happens each time in the vast movements of love, which cannot be arrested or contained! Only because we exclude death in a sudden fit of reflection has it become increasingly strange for us and, since we kept it at such a distance, something hostile.

It is conceivable that it is infinitely closer to us than life itself. . . . What do we know of it?! Our efforts (this has become increasingly clear to me over the years, and my work has perhaps only this *one* meaning and mission, to bear witness to this realization, which so often unexpectedly overwhelms me ever more impartially and independently . . . perhaps more visionarily, if that does not sound too proud) . . . our efforts, I believe, can aim *only* at assuming the *unity* of life and death so that it may gradually prove itself to us. Since we are so prejudiced *against* death we do not succeed in releasing it from its disfigurations ... I urge you to believe, my dear Countess, that death is a *friend,* our most profound and perhaps the only friend who is never, ever misled by our actions and vacillations ... And I do *not mean this,* of course, in that sentimental, romantic sense of renouncing or opposing life, but it is our friend especially *then* when we most passionately and profoundly consent to being here, to change, to nature and to love. Life always says at once: Yes and No. Death (I implore you to believe it!) is the true yes-sayer. It says *only:* Yes. Before eternity.

Just think of the "Sleeping Tree." How good that I just thought of it. Think of all of the small pictures and their inscriptions—*how,* in your youthful innocent faith, you always recognized and affirmed *both* in the world: the sleeping and the waking, the bright and the dark, the voice and the silence ... *la présence et l'absence.* All the presumed opposites which converge somewhere in one point where they sing the hymn of their union—and this place is, for the time being, our heart!

Always steadfastly yours,
Rilke

To Countess Margot
Sizzo-Noris-Crouy

April 12, 1923
Château de Muzot sur Sierre, Valais

My dear honorable Countess:

It is time for me to send some personal words after the two small packages that I mailed last week. Above all, I want to say thank you for the kindness and friendship of your letter dated March 10. You should know that I have read it again and again to be close to you and to completely understand and grasp the current condition of your pain. It must be very deep since you have been able to penetrate into its far, becalmed reaches (few people, simply because they mistrust pain, ever get there—), and it also must be very truthful since you have been able to pursue it into its most physical symptoms and experience its two extremes: completely in the mental sphere, where it so infinitely exceeds us that we experience it as nothing any longer except silence, a pause, as an interval of our nature, and then again, suddenly, at its opposite end, where it is like bodily suffering, a clumsy, utterly point- less children's pain that makes us moan. But is it not won- derful (and is it not somehow an act of maternal care) to be given in this way a tour of the contrasts of one's own nature? And indeed you often experience it as a kind of initiation and induction into the *Whole* and as if nothing evil, nothing deadly in an evil sense could happen to you ever again after you have gone through this elementary suffering just once in a pure and truthful manner. I have often told myself that this was the urge or (if one may put it like this) the sacred ploy of the martyrs to demand to get done with pain, even the most horrific pain, the excess of all pain—that which otherwise spreads randomly in smaller or larger doses of bodily and mental suffering over the course of a life and blends into its moments. They wanted to summon and conjure up this entire capacity for suffering *at once* so that after it, past such endurance, there would be nothing but beatitude, the uninterrupted beatitude of beholding God, which noth- ing can disturb any longer when all has been overcome. The loss that now casts its deep shadow over you is also a task to endure and a matter of *coming to terms with* all of the suffering that may befall us—for once the mother leaves us, we lose all protection. You have to undergo the terrible process of becoming more resilient. But in return ... (and you have also begun to feel *this* already) in return the power of protection now becomes yours, and all the gentleness which until now you had been able to *receive* will blossom more and more inside of you into *your* new capacity to share it as something—inherited and acquired unspeakably, at the deepest price—of your own.

I have suggested to you more than once that I am increasingly motivated in my life and in my work by the aspiration to correct everywhere our old repressions that have distanced and gradually alienated us from the secrets which would let us live out of infinite abundance. People have been scared and terrified by life's horrors; but is there anything sweet and wonderful that has not, from time to time, worn *this* mask, which is one of horror? Life itself—and we know nothing else besides it—isn't it horrific? But as soon as we admit its horror (not as an opponent, for *how* could we measure up to it? but somehow trusting that this very horror is entirely *ours* and merely at this moment still too great, too expansive, too ungraspable for our hearts which are still learning), as soon as we affirm life's most frightening horror at the risk of dying (that is, of our excess!), we gain a hint of the greatest bliss that is ours at this price. The person who has not at some point accepted with ultimate resolve and even rejoiced in the absolute horror of life will never take possession of the unspeakable powers vested in our existence. He moves along the edge and, once the decision is made, will have been neither one of the living nor one of the dead.

To prove the *unity* of horror and bliss, these two faces of the same divinity, indeed of this *single* face that presents itself differently depending on the distance and disposition from which we perceive it: That is the essential meaning and conception of my two books, one of which, the *Sonnets to Orpheus,* you now hold already in your kind hands.

Over Easter I had some friends here to whom I read (for the third time now) the poems out loud. Each time I discovered how much a few small and casual remarks can aid in their understanding. But for that they must be read out loud in person. While I was thus reading the other evening I thought of you, dearest Countess, and I was filled with such a strong desire to look through this book with you, page by page, in order to present to you each individual poem in all of its strength. I now know there is not a single one that is not clear and rich with meaning, even if a few of them are placed so close to the unspeakable secret that they cannot be explained but only . . . endured. But I learned how much my voice unwittingly contributes to their explication if only because it still reverberates with the whole mystery of their creation, which is then transmitted to the listener via indescribable vibrations.

If I am not mistaken, I have already told you that these peculiar *Sonnets to Orpheus* had not been planned or anticipated. They arrived, sometimes *many* in one day (the book's first part was created in about three days) without warning in February of last year while I was actually trying to regain my focus to continue those other poems, the great *Duino Elegies*. I could do nothing but accept, without altering or resisting, the dictation of what had built up inside of me. I also only understood after some time that and how these stanzas refer to the figure of Vera Knoop who passed away at the age of eighteen or nineteen. I had not known her well and saw her only a few times in life, when she was still a child, even if then I had certainly been strangely intrigued and moved. Even though I did not put them in this order (with the exception of a few poems at the beginning of the second part, all the sonnets remain in the chronological sequence of their creation) it ended up that in each of the two parts only the *pen*ultimate poems refer explicitly to Vera, or address or evoke her figure.

This beautiful child who first took up dancing and caused a stir among all those who saw her back then, thanks to her body's and mind's innate art of movement and transformation—unexpectedly explained to her mother that she could not or did not want to dance any longer (this happened right at the end of childhood). Her body changed in strange ways and became, without losing its beautiful Eastern shape, strangely heavy and massive ... (this was already the beginning of the mysterious glandular disease which would then so rapidly lead to her death). During the time that remained, Vera took up music and finally confined herself to drawing, as if the dance she had had to give up found ever quieter and more discreet expression through her . . . I knew her father, Gerhard Ouckama Knoop, who had spent the greatest part of his life as an engineer at Knoop's great textile factories in Moscow. Later he had to retire from this position due to a strange heart condition that stumped his doctors. He moved with his wife and two daughters (Vera was the younger one) to Germany, and still had time to write several books which have not remained unknown but perhaps do not give an adequate sense of this modest man's absolutely unique way of experiencing life. His final years must have been full of fantastic insights and realizations, and the process of his dying, perhaps helped by the particular condition of his heart, was a complete detachment from the here and now in an indescribable purification of his spirit. ... He died *knowingly*, and in some ways flooded by insights into eternity, and his final breath arrived on a breeze from the angels' wings he had set trembling. ... I did not know him well either, since in Paris, where he visited me only once, I did not have an opportunity for closer contact with him . . . But from the beginning we had shared the kind of instinctual trust and mutual joy that does not need further proof, and which perhaps originated in the same source as the startling inspiration that now so incomprehensibly inspired me to erect this gravestone for young Vera!

It would be too much if I now tried to offer comments on a few individual sonnets, and I also would like to keep this as a reason for a future meeting. I thought it justified to share these hints with you so that you may at least read the book correctly. They will make some things clearer and be a gentle guide for your reading hours.

It's perhaps also useful to know that Sonnet XVI (of the first part), page 22, is addressed to a dog: I intentionally did not want to make this explicit, since that would have seemed almost again like the exclusion (or at least differentiation) of the creature that I specifically wanted to absorb completely into our experience. (I wonder whether one can surmise or would have guessed that here a dog is being addressed?)

I conclude, honorable Countess. The anemones! I wonder what you thought of them (if they reached you in still somewhat recognizable shape). Last year someone told me that this dark-purple furry kind of pasqueflower grew *only* in the Swiss canton of Valais. As inexperienced as I am unfortunately in botany, I was happy to believe it.

But today someone passed through who called the small flower with degrading familiarity "cow-" or even "kitchen-bell" and assured me *que c'était tout ce qu'il y a de plus commun* [that it was most common]. Well, that alone would not make them any less beautiful but it still got me wondering, since the way in which it appears here as the first growth in the rocky terrain, enveloped in the care of its silvery fur to shelter it from any mishap, it really appears rare and noble. Had you known it? Does it grow like this in Hungary?

I had music here around Easter—that's the one thing I still have to tell you—wonderful music. It was really an event for me since so rarely I am able to be receptive to music (and perhaps I don't even wish or dare to be open to it more frequently). My Swiss friends brought along a very young violinist who, they assured me, is already considered among the best and most extraordinary artists on her instrument.

She played Bach for me for three days, almost exclusively Bach—and *how, how!* She handled her violin with such maturity and such certainty, and with such resolve. (*This* is how fates and lives would have to run their course, but this kind of taut strength [and this precision], which harbors and shelters gentleness inside of it, only exists in a realm without fate.) The young artist, Alma Moodie (Scottish on her father's side, Irish on her mother's, born in Australia, currently working with [the violinist and teacher Carl] Flesch in Berlin), is soon going on a concert tour in Romania . . . If she passes through Hungary to play in Pest and you can arrange it, *please*, go and listen to her.

I gave her (for Romania) the delightful book by Princess Marthe Bibesco, *Isvor, le pays des saules* ["Isvor, Land of Willows"], in two volumes. A book filled with deep experiences of the local people's lives and sentiments which have been passed down through ancient traditions, with pages of purest perception and poetry: Would you like me to send it to you? (I think it is difficult to obtain French books abroad.)

I remain your humble servant and gratefully yours,

Rilke

To Claire Goll

———

The German-French writer Claire Goll (née Studer, 1901–1977; Rilke called her Liliane) was married to the poet Yvan Goll (1892–1951). She met Rilke for the first time in 1918 after sending him a book of her poems. They had a brief affair and maintained a friendship thereafter. The letter refers to the death of her father.

OCTOBER 22, 1923
Currently: Bern, Hôtel Bellevue

Liliane,

Before writing this to you I had torn up another letter that I had written two nights ago, since I do not feel like telling you anything "general" at the moment when you demand my empathy and attention. And yet, tell me, *how* to find those particular words that will be valid exactly for you, since I have learned only via the abbreviated announcement of the type of affliction that now puts you to an immensely difficult test.

You see, I think that now, since you are confronted for

the first time with having to suffer death in the death of the person who is so infinitely close to you, all of death (somehow more than only your own, possible death), that now is the moment when you are most capable of truly perceiving and recognizing the pure secret which, believe me, is not that of death but of life.

Now it is necessary, in an unspeakably and inexhaustibly magnanimous gesture of pain, to include death in life, all of death, since through someone precious to you it has moved within your reach (and you have become related to it). Make it part of life as something no longer to be rejected, no longer denied. Pull it toward you with all your strength, this horrific thing, and as long as you cannot do that, *pretend* that you are comfortable and familiar with it. Don't scare it off by being scared of it (like everyone else). Interact with it or, if that is still too much of an effort for you, at least hold still so that it can get very close, that always chased-off creature of death, and let it cuddle up to you. For this, you see, is what death has become for us: something always chased away that no longer had a chance of revealing itself to us. If at the moment when it hurts and devastates us, death were treated by even the simplest person with some familiarity (and not with horror), what confessions would it share when it— finally—passed over to him! Only a small moment of open-mindedness toward it, a brief suppression of prejudice, and it is ready to share infinite intimacies that would overwhelm our tendency to endure it with trembling hesitation. Patience, Liliane, nothing but: patience.

Once you have been granted access to the Whole and thus been initiated, you solemnly celebrate your own true independence. You become more protective and more capable of granting protection exactly to the extent that you have lost and now lack protection. The solitude into which you were cast so violently makes you capable of balancing out the loneliness of others to exactly the same degree. And as your own sense of difficulty is concerned, you will soon realize that it has posited a new measure for your existence and a new standard for your suffering and endurance.

I offer a bit of advice, Liliane; I am trying nothing more but to be close to you with these simple words. On some later occasion you will tell me whether they were of any use, for nobody comes close to true assistance and consolation, except by an act of grace.

Rainer

(P.S. After some longer travels, a spa treatment, and other changes, I am on my way back to Muzot.)

To Magdalena Schwammberger

*Magdalena Schwammberger (1892–1979) was from Burg-
dorf near Bern, Switzerland. She met Rilke after one of
his public readings in Switzerland in 1919.*

DECEMBER 23, 1923
Château de Muzot s / Sierre
(Valais)

My dear miss:

Do I need to say it? Do I need to assure you? I read
your recent letter with the same attentiveness and joy as
the earlier, first one. If I didn't respond, it was due to a lot
of things I had needed to catch up on (returning to Muzot
quite late in the year) and, to tell you everything, also
because I have not been well.

I want to thank you for adding to the trust you've
placed in me, for your new contributions . . . and not least
of all for how you let me feel that what I had tried to tell
you recently indeed found you receptive. Alas, I know
that these consolations amount to so little, for they are

quickly used up and the heartache incessantly replenishes on its own.

But your new letter proves to me that you are able to lift your gaze up and above it, toward many important and lasting matters. And this means that you are not in danger of becoming trapped in an impoverishing daily bitterness. For people who are permanently caught in sorrow in this way there is only *one* liberation: to lift suffering itself up into one's own gaze and from there let it assist one's vision. I suspect that for some time now you have had this realization on your own, and that a few times already you have had the experience of perceiving more richly and deeply things which happen or are shown to you, precisely on the basis of your sorrow.

I am quite happy that I am now in the position (while my letter has to remain all too brief) to speak with you differently and with more validity: by means of the enclosed book, along with which a few petals of your beautiful roses are also returning to you.

Please accept my warmest regards, also for Christmas!

R. M. Rilke

And definitely: When I visit Bern at some point we should arrange to meet there or in Burgdorf. I am looking forward to it.

To Rudolf F. Burckhardt

Burckhardt (1877–1964) was a Swiss art historian and the conservator of the Basel Historical Museum from 1908 to 1926. His correspondence with Rilke began after their first encounter in 1919. The "three pale brothers" in the letter may refer to a fourteenth-century jewel identified by Burkhardt. Sonnet XXI in Sonnets to Orpheus *also refers to the medieval tapestry of a garden of love mentioned in the letter.*

April 14, 1924
Muzot s/Sierre (Valais)

My dear Rudolf F. Burckhardt,

When I address you in this effort of innermost concentration, I become aware that nothing has been forgotten of the many good things that you were able to arrange for me since our first encounter (at a festive occasion where the "three pale brothers" played a role). I continue to remember those hours in Venice and our correspondence about the tapestry of the garden of love, and I think of all of those moments as more than only the circumstances of verifiable memory. All of us who have learned patience and sensitivity from things which have survived and long been admired probably share *this* sense that destiny's vagaries pass to us in more ways than only via what is real or visible. How should we not, when it truly matters, understand such experiences as both a kind of assistance and the unspoken sense that we who experience this are placed within a greater Whole from which we cannot be removed? Yes: The more someone has been able to recognize here, the more separations and farewells he will have had to accomplish through the course of his life. But I often feel as if these separations and departures would all be affirmations again in an open world, and that they would be called something else there.

Yours,
Rainer Maria Rilke

TO CATHERINE POZZI

Catherine Pozzi (1882–1934) was a French poet and essay-
ist. Her correspondence (in French) with Rilke took place
during 1924–1925 after a first meeting arranged by the poet
Paul Valéry (1871–1945). Her poetry was published post-
humously. Henri de Régnier, who is mentioned in the let-
ter, was a French symbolist poet (1864–1936) and married
to Marie de Régnier, a poet and novelist who used the pen
name Gérard d'Houville.

AUGUST 21, 1924
Château de Muzot
s/Sierre (Valais) Switzerland

Dear esteemed friend:

You were truly in danger—I could imagine that was
what made me stop in Bern to write to you. But the whole
time I was writing this letter I did not feel at all like telling you anything, and instead there was a sudden urge to
quickly rush to you and be close to you: It was like a sup-
pressed trip. But what a stupid accident that has cast you
among the worst dangers. It is a series of bad coincidences

(a mosquito bite, food poisoning by a moldy casserole, etc.) that most compromises the order which I would like to discover. It seems to me like the strange occurrence of a nasty disease which, to excite the nosy neighbors, attacks anyone at all, at any time, to find out what will happen next! And that surgeon: In spite of your weakness, are you strong enough not to hate him? I can say without feeling embarrassed: I hate him!

I was quite envious of Henri de Régnier, who was able to visit you, not that I was feeling capable of offering any sort of "consolation" that would have matched his, but because I so much wish to speak with you in person. My pen has grown a bit cold and exhausted from using it apart from my actual work. It seems to me that this dual use, which is already so damaging to writing, makes it sometimes entirely uncertain. Because what one expresses immediately, just in order to communicate something, is so very different from the lasting expression of art that needs to be captured and accepted with full consciousness in order to make itself be understood much later. And the pen, between those two tasks, vacillates and hesitates. So many times I envied Rodin his docile and relaxed earthen clay, which cannot be used to say hello or to order a meal!

Finally, what I am displaying is perhaps nothing but the symptom of a great fatigue that seems to weigh me down after an extremely long period of uninterrupted solitude. If you were to ask me, I believe I would agree that I am rather unhappy at the moment but nonetheless find myself at the bottom of definitive happiness. I am going through a bad moment (which drags on), but what good is it to talk about it; it isn't during that moment, in any case, that I am writing to you.

I imagine your life (and you always give me the most convincing proof), in spite of all the bad, to have been good and victorious. Already in your childhood and early youth, you seem to have been surrounded by wisdom and understanding. The elders in your life had decided (and were able) to lead you toward life and to prepare you to relate to it with dignity, and you have had—in body and soul—the most fortunate gift of being able to accept their generous suggestions. How different that was for us (with some rare exceptions) in Austria, where everyone seemed to take pleasure in pointing out obstacles. Ultimately it was almost a constructive idea, in that contradictory country, to seek out the impossibilities and rejoice in them. The young generation just managed on its own under this unhealthy regime of obstinate and disillusioned bureaucrats.

The contradictions that are found in my writings: Do they have their roots in that past which I have not been able to correct even through my most clear-eyed efforts?

Probably, for in life I also often feel quite advanced in certain areas while in others I remain less knowledgeable than the simplest person. In life, such contrasts are difficult to reconcile and can at any moment become disastrous. In art, if you have the time to persevere and create an entire, uninterrupted work, such oppositions, even those of ideas, are necessary and can finally constitute a kind of alternating rhythm. I believe, moreover, that these more or less provisional contradictions which you have noticed in my verses are not so much *there* where you place them right now. I believe, for example, that it would be not too difficult for us to agree about the two poems (Sonnets XII and XIII) which propose to consent absolutely to the changes and transformations of our conditions. The most profound experiences of my life all converge to make me acknowledge death as another part of that trajectory whose vertiginous curve we follow without being able to come to a halt even for a moment. I feel more and more drawn, from my provisional position, to agree with that Whole where life and death penetrate each other and incessantly mix. The Angel of my affirmations (*der Engel des Jasagens* [*The Angel of Saying Yes*]), turns a radiant face toward death. Although life needs so much else, it is death above all, death *itself,* weighed down by so many bad suspicions, that I would like to rehabilitate by putting it back in that central spot it has never left but from which we have averted our eyes. I feel compelled to demonstrate that it is one of the great treasures of that formidable Whole of which life is perhaps only the smallest part, even though life is already so rich on its own that it surpasses all of our means and all of our measures. Such complete agreement with change must be grounded in events filled with constancy and permanence—and indeed I too can affirm that I feel "so much the same in spirit and body." If I infinitely agree with the necessary transformations and all of the farewells which a greater rhythm imposes on us, that is because for me the fog of all these changes begins to turn transparent, thanks to our flame which passes through them without ever being extinguished. But I stop here. I venture nothing but conjectures, and I will not claim to explain my poems. I would like to believe, instead, that they think for me and will succeed in enlightening me!

I am preparing for my return: again to Grisons, Ragaz, and the surrounding areas, unless there is an unforeseen change in my projects. After that it will be (perhaps): Paris! I share this with you in secret because such a beautiful project should stay locked up so that it is truly new at the moment of its happy realization. It is an indescribable joy for me to think that one day it will be permitted for me to visit you as if it were completely natural and not at all a chapter of a miracle. Perhaps one day I could meet there again Madame Gérard d'Houville. I have known for a long time how wonderful she is. (Once, many years ago, I noticed from my window in the Palazzo Valmarana in Venice, how she crossed the small Campo de San Vio alongside M. de Régnier.) It seems to me that you promise me the continuation of so many lines which happy circumstances had begun to trace earlier. Thank you!

Rilke

P.S. Before I return I will send you my copy of the *Elegies* (the book which finally infinitely *consents*) to exchange it later for your definitive copy of the current edition.

To Witold Hulewicz

The poet, literary critic, and publisher Witold Hulewicz (1895–1941) translated Rilke's writings into Polish. The two writers' first meeting, in Switzerland in the early 1920s, was followed by a friendship and long correspondence. Rilke's Book of Hours *appeared in 1905,* The New Poems *in 1907 and 1908,* The Notebook of Malte Laurids Brigge *in 1910, and* The Sonnets to Orpheus *and* Duino Elegies *in 1923.*

[Sierre, November 13, 1925]

And is it *I* who may offer the correct explanation for the *Elegies?* They reach out infinitely beyond me. I regard them to be a further elaboration of those essential premises that were already given in the *Book of Hours,* that tentatively played with the world-image in both parts of the *New Poems,* and that then in *Malte,* contracted in conflict, strike back into life and there almost become proof that this life, so suspended above an abyss, is impossible. In the *Elegies,* based on the same conditions, life becomes possible again.

Indeed, here it receives that ultimate affirmation to which young Malte, though on the correct and difficult path of his *"longues études"* [extensive studies], could not yet lead it. *The affirmation of life-and-death appears as one in the* Elegies. To admit one without the other would be, as the *Elegies* let us experience and celebrate, a limitation which in the end shuts out all that is infinite. Death is the *side of life* that is turned away from us and upon which we do not cast our light: We must try to achieve the greatest awareness of our existence that is at home in *both unbounded realms* and is *inexhaustibly nourished by them.* The true figure of life extends through *both* spheres, the blood of the greatest circulation courses through both: *There is neither a here and now nor a beyond but the great unity* where the beings which surpass us, the angels, are at home. And now to the matter of the problem of love, in this world expanded by its greater half, in this world only now *complete* and only now *healed.* I am surprised that the *Sonnets to Orpheus,* which are at least as *"difficult"* and filled with the same essence, are not more helpful for you in understanding the *Elegies.* These latter poems were begun in 1912 (at Duino), continued in Spain and Paris (in fragments) until 1914; the war interrupted this, my greatest work, altogether; when I dared in 1922 to take them up again (here), the new *Elegies* and their conclusion were preceded by a few days by the *Sonnets to Orpheus,* which imposed themselves tempestuously (and which had *not* been in my plan). They are, as it cannot be otherwise, of the same "birth" as the *Elegies* and the fact that they appeared suddenly, without a conscious effort of my will, in connection with a girl who had died young, brings them even closer to the source of their origin. The connection is yet another relation to the center of *that* realm whose depth and influence we, everywhere unbounded, share with the dead and those yet to come. We, who live here and now, are not for a moment satisfied in the time-world nor confined in it; we incessantly flow over and over to those who preceded us, to our origin, and to those who seemingly come after us. In that greatest "open" world all *are*, not really "simultaneously," since the dropping away of time results in a state where they all *are*. Transience everywhere plunges into a deep being. Thus all of the configurations of the here and now are to be used not only in a time-bound way but, as far as we can accomplish that, to be integrated into those superior meanings of which we are a part. But *not in the Christian sense* (from which I am moving away ever more passionately), but in a purely earthy, blissfully earthy consciousness, we must introduce what we see and touch *here* into the wider and widest orbit. Not into a beyond whose shadow darkens the earth, but into a whole, into *the whole*. Nature, the things of our daily interactions and use, are provisional and perishable. But as long as we are here, they are *our* property and our friendship, co-conspirators in our distress and joy just as they have already been the familiars of our forebears. So it is important not only not to disparage and degrade everything that exists in the here and now—rather, especially because of their provisional character, which they share with us, these phenomena and things should be understood and transformed by us with our innermost sense. Transformed? Yes, for it is our task to imprint this provisional, perishable earth so deeply, so painfully and passionately in ourselves that its reality shall arise in us again "invisibly." We are the bees of the Universe. *Nous butinons éperdument le miel du visible, pour l'accumuler dans la grande ruche d'or de l'Invisible.* [We wildly gather the honey of the visible, in order to store it in the great golden hive of the Invisible.] The *Elegies* show us, by way of this effort of the continual transformations of the beloved visible and tangible into the invisible vibration and excitation of our own nature, that new frequencies of vibration are introduced into the vibrating spheres of the universe. (Since the different elements in the cosmos are only different exponents of vibration, we prepare, in this way, not only intensities of a mental kind but, who knows, new bodies, metals, nebulae, and constellations.) And this activity is curiously supported and urged on by the ever more rapid vanishing of so many visible things that will no longer be replaced. Even for our grandparents a "house," a "well," a familiar tower, their very clothes, and even their coat were infinitely more, infinitely more intimate, and almost any object was for them a vessel in which they encountered the human and added to the store of the human. Now, from America, empty indifferent things are pouring across, make-believe things, *mock-ups of life* . . . A house, in the American sense, an American apple, or a grapevine over there has *nothing* in common with the house, the fruit, the grape into which had entered the hopes and thoughtful- ness of our forefathers . . . The things that are animated and *share in our knowledge* because they were truly experienced, are running out and can no longer be replaced. We *are per- haps the last ones who will still have known such things.* On us rests the responsibility not only of preserving *their* mem- ory (that would be little and unreliable), but their human and lares-like worth. ("Lares" in the sense of the guardian deities of the home.) The earth has no other way out than to become invisible: only *in* us who with a part of our na- ture partake of the invisible and who have (at least) some stock in it, and who can increase our holdings in the invis- ible during our sojourn here. In us alone can this intimate and lasting transformation be consummated that turns the visible into something invisible which no longer depends on seeing or touching it, just as our own destiny grows *at once more present and invisible* in us. The *Elegies* posit this norm for our existence: They affirm and celebrate this con- sciousness. They cautiously integrate it into its traditions by referring back to ancient transmissions and the rumors of such transmissions to justify this supposition and even invoke a preknowledge of such relations in the Egyptian cult of the dead. (Although the "Land of Lamentation" through which the older "lamentation" leads the young dead [in *Duino Elegies*] is *not* to be *identified with Egypt* but is only, in a sense, a mirroring of the Nile region in the desert clarity of the consciousness of the dead.) When one makes the mistake of applying *Catholic* concepts of death, of the beyond and of eternity to the *Elegies* or *Sonnets,* one gets entirely away from their point of departure and prepares for an ever more basic misunderstanding. The "angel" of the *Elegies* has nothing to do with the angel of the Christian heaven (it is closer to the angel figures of Islam). The angel of the *Elegies* is that creature in whom the transformation of the visible into the invisible, which we accomplish, appears already consummated. For the angel of the *Elegies,* all past towers and palaces exist because they have been long invisible, and the still standing towers and bridges of our existence are already invisible although (for us) they still persist physically. The angel of the *Elegies* is that being which vouches for the recognition of the invisible at a higher order of reality.—That is why he is "terrible" for us since we, its lovers and transformers, still cling to the visible after all.—All the worlds of the universe plunge into the invisible as their next-deeper reality; *a few stars intensify immediately and expire in the infinite consciousness of the angels. Others depend on beings who slowly and laboriously transform them, and in whose terrors and ecstasies they reach their next invisible realization.* We *are,* let it be emphasized once more, *in the sense of the* Elegies, *we are the transformers of the earth. Our entire existence, the flights and sudden plunges of our love, everything qualifies us for this task* (beside which there exists, essentially, no other). (The *Sonnets* show some details of this activity which here appears under the name and protection of a dead girl whose incompletion and innocence holds open the entrance to the grave so that she, having gone from us, belongs to those powers that keep one half of life fresh and turned toward the other, opened up like a wound.) The *Elegies* and *Sonnets* support each other constantly, and I consider it an infinite grace that I was permitted to fill both sails with the same breath: the small, rust-colored sail of the *Sonnets* and the gigantic white canvas of the *Elegies.*

May you, dear friend, find some advice and elucidation in this letter and, for the rest, rely on yourself for help. For: I do not know whether I could ever say more.

Yours,
R. M. Rilke

Rainer Maria Rilke:
Life and Works

1875   December 4. René Karl Wilhelm Johann Josef Maria Rilke is born in Prague, in the Austro-Hungarian Empire, to rail inspector Joseph and his wife, Sophie (Phia) Rilke (born Entz).

1882   Attends elementary school of a Catholic order.

1884   Parents separate. Rilke is raised by his mother.

1886   Admission to military youth academy of St. Pölten.

1890   Attends a military academy in Mährisch-Weisskirchen (now Hranice, Czech Republic).

1891   Admission to trade school in Linz.

1892   Prepares privately for baccalaureate in Prague.

1894   First collection of poems, *Lives and Songs*.

1895   Baccalaureate. University studies in Prague (art history, philosophy, and literature).

1896   University studies in Munich.

1897   Begins a four-year love affair with Lou Andreas-Salomé in Munich. Moves to Berlin.

1898 Travels to Italy. Since August in Berlin.
      Publication of the collection of novels and
      sketches, *Am Leben hin (Near Life)*.

1899 First travels to Russia with Andreas-Salomé. Visits
      in Moscow with Leonid Pasternak and Leo Tolstoy.

1900 Second visit to Russia with Andreas-Salomé. Visit
      to the artists' colony in Worpswede (northern
      Germany) at the invitation of painter Heinrich
      Vogeler.

1901 Marriage to sculptor Clara Westhoff. Birth of his
      only child, Ruth.

1902 Publication of *The Book of Images*. Trip to Paris.
      Publication of the commissioned monograph
      Auguste Rodin.

1903 Travels to Viareggio, Rome, Florence, Munich,
      Paris, and other locations in Europe.

1904 Visit to Sweden.

1905 Worpswede and Paris. Rilke lives as the assistant to
      Auguste Rodin in Meudon (near Paris).
      Publication of *The Book of Hours*.

1906 Death of Rilke's father. End of the relationship
      with Rodin. Rilke moves to Paris. Travels to
      Belgium and Capri.

1907 Publication of *New Poems*. Love affair with Mimi
      Romanelli.

1908 With his family in Bremen. Travels to Berlin,
     Munich, Rome, Capri, Florence. *The New Poems:
     Second Part.*

1910 Travels to Algiers and Tunis. Publication of *The
     Notebooks of Malte Laurids Brigge.*

1911 Travels to Egypt, Italy, Bohemia, Germany, and
     France. Rilke spends part of the winter at Duino
     Castle (owned by the Thurn und Taxis family) in
     northern Italy.

1912 Travels to Spain.

1914 Rilke finds himself in Munich at the beginning of
     the war and as a citizen of the Austro-Hungarian
     Empire is not permitted to return to Paris. He
     loses most of his belongings that remain in Paris.

1915 Encounter with Sigmund Freud in Munich. Rilke
     is drafted into the Austro-Hungarian army, despite
     attempts to defer.

1916 Call to active duty, then service in the war archives
     in Vienna. Return to Munich.

1918 Meeting and love affair with the poet Claire
     Studer (later the wife of poet Yvan Goll). After the
     dissolution of the Austro-Hungarian Empire, Rilke
     automatically becomes a Czech citizen.

1919 Meeting with Andreas-Salomé. Visit to
     Switzerland from Munich. Rilke begins his

relationship with the painter Baladine Klossowska, and helps in educating and providing for her two sons, Pierre and Balthasar (later the painter Balthus). Appeals to influential patrons to obtain a residency permit in Switzerland.

1921　Rilke moves into a small stone house, Château de Muzot, near Sierre in the Swiss canton of Valais, which is first rented and then purchased for him by his sponsor Werner Reinhart.

1922　Completion of the *Duino Elegies* and creation of *Sonnets to Orpheus* (both works appear in 1923). Marriage of daughter Ruth.

1923　First stay in a sanatorium in Val-Mont sur Territet near Lake Geneva.

1924　Paul Valéry and Clara Westhoff, among other guests, visit Rilke in Switzerland. Another stay at the clinic in Val-Mont.

1925　January to August in Paris, then back at Muzot. From December at the clinic in Val-Mont.

1926　Return to Muzot in June. From November in Val-Mont, where he receives a diagnosis of leukemia. Rilke dies on December 29 in Val-Mont.

1927　Rilke is buried on January 2 at the cemetery in Raron, in the canton of Valais. In the fall, a six-volume *Collected Works* is published.

A NOTE ON THE AUTHOR

RAINER MARIA RILKE, widely considered to rank among the greatest poets in any language, was born in Prague in 1875. The only child of German-speaking parents, he attended a military boarding academy before studying literature, art history and philosophy at university in both Prague and Munich. Throughout his life he maintained a long, generous correspondence with friends, acquaintances and fans that amounts to around 15,000 letters. Rilke considered these letters to be as important as his poetry, with the most famous selection published posthumously as *Letters to a Young Poet* (1929). In 1901 he married the sculptor Clara Westhoff and had a daughter, Ruth. Both Rilke and his wife, though now separated, moved to Paris in 1902, where Rilke wrote a monograph on the sculptor Auguste Rodin and served for a period as his secretary. Rodin's work had a great effect on Rilke and motivated him to write the *New Poems* (1907, 1908), adding to his other major works of verse in this early period, *The Book of Images* (1902) and *The Book of Hours* (1905). Paris became his main residence and inspired his only novel, *The Notebooks of Malte Laurids Brigge* (1910). Rilke was staying in Munich at the outbreak of World War I and found himself unable to return to Paris. Briefly conscripted to the military in 1916, he moved to Switzerland after the war, completing the *Duino Elegies* and the *Sonnets to Orpheus* in 1922 in a burst of creativity over the span of five days. They are considered one of the most significant poetic achievements in world literature. After a period of ill health, Rilke died from leukaemia in 1926 and was buried in Switzerland.

ULRICH BAER was educated at Harvard and Yale and has been awarded John Simon Guggenheim, DAAD, Paul Getty and Alexander von Humboldt Fellowships. He is Professor of Comparative and German Literature and Photography and Imagining at New York University and has published, among other books, *The Rilke Alphabet, Rilke: Die Prosa* and *Rainer Maria Rilke: Letters on Life.*

A NOTE ON THE TYPE

The principal text of this edition was set in a digitised version of Janson, a typeface that dates from about 1690 and was cut by Nicholas Kis (1650–1702), a Hungarian working in Amsterdam. The original matrices have survived and are held by the Stempel foundry in Germany. Hermann Zapf (b. 1918) redesigned some of the weights and sizes for Stempel, basing his revisions on the original design.